16⁹⁵

Conversations on the
Plurality of Worlds

Conversations
on the Plurality
of Worlds

Bernard le Bovier de Fontenelle

Translation by
H. A. Hargreaves

Introduction by
Nina Rattner Gelbart

UNIVERSITY OF CALIFORNIA PRESS

Berkeley / Los Angeles / London

University of California Press
Berkeley and Los Angeles, California

University of California Press
London, England

Copyright © 1990 by The Regents of the University of California

Library of Congress Cataloging-in-Publication Data

Fontenelle, M. de (Bernard Le Bovier), 1657–1757.
   [Entretiens sur la pluralité des mondes. English]
   Conversations on the plurality of worlds / Bernard le Bovier de
Fontenelle; translation by H. A. Hargreaves; introduction by Nina
Rattner Gelbart.
     p. cm.
   Translation of: Entretiens sur la pluralité des mondes.
   ISBN 0-520-07171-9
   1. Plurality of worlds—Early works to 1800.   I. Title.
QB54.FG13   1990
574.999—dc20   90-31220
                                           CIP

Printed in the United States of America

08   07   06   05   04   03   02   01   00
9 8 7 6 5

The paper used in this publication meets the minimum requirements
of ANSI/NISO Z39.48-1992 (R 1997) (*Permanence of Paper*). ∞

Contents

Introduction

F ontenelle's *Entretiens sur la pluralité des mondes* or *Conversations on the Plurality of Worlds* became an instant best-seller three hundred years ago. But the author, introducing these ideas for the first time to a broad public, courted danger when he wrote his pioneering work in 1686. Less than a century earlier, in 1600, Giordano Bruno had been burned at the stake for, among other offenses, desacrilizing the Earth by suggesting the possibility of multiple inhabited worlds in the universe. Only fifty years before Fontenelle wrote, Galileo had lost his freedom and had been placed under permanent house arrest for writing on daring astronomical theories. So while much of Fontenelle sounds matter-of-fact to us—his talk of a boundless universe, his speculations on intelligent extraterrestrial and extragalactic life, his discussion of space travel—we have to remember that publishing his book three centuries ago was very risky business. The ideas he was bandying about were bold, controversial, even forbidden. As they had been scarcely known to the average reader before he explained and disseminated them, these astonishing ideas suddenly became the rage. Since its first appearance in French, there have been approximately one hundred editions of the *Entretiens*. It has been translated into English, Danish, Dutch, German, Greek, Italian, Polish, Russian, Spanish, and Swedish. Thus there is a very real sense in which Fontenelle's work spread the word, encouraged the curiosity, and created the international audience that this subject still enjoys today.

But why were these cosmological ideas once dangerous? To be properly persuaded that writers expounded on this subject at immense personal cost, or at least at great risk, we have to familiarize ourselves with the scientific theories and climate of Fontenelle's day. Then we will be better able to understand how the notions in his book threatened received wisdom on the subject.

The prevailing view of the universe, since the days of Aristotle and Ptolemy, was that Earth stood at the center of a relatively small, bounded, finite world, with the Moon, the Sun, and all the other planets and stars spinning about it. The sublunar region, composed of the four "elements," earth, air, fire and water, obeyed one set of physical laws, while the Moon, Sun, and planets, made of a different, immutable material and embedded in crystalline spheres, proceeded in combinations of circular motion, obeying a different physics. This gave humankind a very special position, as the noblest creatures in the central spot, around which the celestial bodies and the very heavens revolved. During the Middle Ages, this pagan view of the universe had needed to be reconciled with the teachings of the Church, a job accomplished by the great intellectual synthesis called Scholasticism, and especially by the writings of Thomas Aquinas. Once Aristotle's cosmology had thus been rendered acceptable, the Church endorsed this picture wholeheartedly, as it made Earth the apple of God's eye, a fitting stage on which the human drama of salvation could be played out. From the astronomical point of view this cosmology had its problems; observations of the skies revealed anomalies—we know now that they are due to Earth's motion—which did not fit neatly into the scheme. For example, the planets, watched from Earth, seemed to slow down, stop, and even go backward, a difficult thing to explain if nature moved in putatively orderly circles. But the appeal of this view of the world had become so great on theological and philosophical grounds that for centuries such objections were overruled, and were even mathematically accommodated in increasingly complex diagrams of the heavens constructed to "save the phenomena."

In 1543, Nicholas Copernicus published his *On the Revolutions of the Heavenly Spheres,* a huge, ponderous Latin tome that exploded the Ptolemaic world view, suggesting instead a heliocentric or Sun-centered universe, with the Moon still revolving about Earth, but Earth, like all the other planets, now spinning around the central Sun. Copernicus's ideas, displacing and demoting the Earth as they did, were radically new and different, and eventually caused a tremendous crisis, though this inevitable reaction was delayed for a while. Copernicus himself was on his deathbed when the work was published. A Lutheran clergyman, Osiander, had written a disclaimer in the book, to the effect that it was merely a computational scheme intended to remedy observational anomalies and not a true representation of the universe or of the actual paths of the planets. Also the work was long, forbidding, full of mathematical equations, and written in the scholarly tongue of Latin so that only those trained in the Church or university could read it. Those who did read it were thrown into turmoil, because the notion of a moving Earth seemed to contradict passages in the Bible. This led to questions about the interpretation of Scripture, whether it should be taken literally or understood metaphorically, and who had the authority to determine its real and allegorical meanings. Some Protestants attempted to make the new astronomy compatible with their reading of biblical texts. Counter-Reformation Catholics, after the Council of Trent, and especially the increasingly influential Jesuits, were opposed to Copernicanism and upheld the literalism of Holy Writ.

Copernicus's ideas, however, were soon to set in motion a chain reaction of revolutionary astronomical research that could not be stopped however hard Christian authorities tried. A Danish astronomer named Tycho Brahe, while not persuaded by Copernicus's arguments, nonetheless realized that ancient astronomical tables were inadequate to resolve the dispute, and set up his own island observatory, monitored round the clock by his students, who provided new, accurate information on celestial movements. Tycho studied comets, which appeared to cross through the crystalline spheres and thus cast doubt on their existence, and observed a supernova, the creation of a new star, another impossible phenomenon in the immutable heavens of Aristotle. Unable to accept either Ptolemy or Copernicus, Tycho came up with his own compromise system. Meanwhile young Johannes Kepler, attracted by Tycho's new astronomical data, had come to work with him. In his study of the planet Mars, Kepler arrived at a staggering conclusion: the orbits of planets could not be reduced to a combination of circles, as had been believed since the ancient Greeks, but were elliptical. Kepler's new laws of planetary motion were buried deep in long rambling writings, and although somewhat known, they would later be appreciated and made familiar by Isaac Newton, whose work they inspired.

Now the ideas of Copernicus, Tycho, and Kepler, though extremely important, remained virtually unknown to the literate public until Galileo's telescopic discoveries of 1609, published in his *Sidereal Messenger* of 1610. The telescope had recently been invented in Holland, and was being advertised and used primarily as a navigational and military tool, but Galileo turned it toward the heavens, and what he saw there altered the course of the history of science forever. He discovered, for the first time, clear observational evidence for Copernicus's system. He saw that the Moon was like a "dead Earth," not the pristine ethereal body of Aristotle's scheme. He saw sunspots, which also contradicted the immutability of the heavens. He saw that Jupiter had moons, thus exemplifying a solar system in miniature. He saw the phases of Venus, changes in its shape which would have been impossible in the geocentric system where, stuck between the Sun and Earth, Venus should always appear a crescent. He saw that the so-called "fixed stars," supposedly the tight outer boundary of the world, were hardly magnified at all, and must, therefore, be immeasurably more distant than had previously been believed. He saw no evidence whatever of any crystalline spheres holding up the planets.

Galileo spent the next two decades biding his time about most of this, continuing to work but publishing little. In 1616 the Catholic Church made an official condemnation of Copernicanism as false and needing to be expurgated (the euphemistic word was "corrected"), and Galileo thought discretion the better part of valor. But when a friend of his, Cardinal Barberini, became Pope Urban VIII, he mistakenly believed he could finally speak freely of the new astronomy. In 1632, he wrote about it in the form of a conversation and in the vernacular Italian in his delightful *Dialogue Concerning the Two Chief World Systems*. (This was doubtless an inspiration for Fontenelle, who wrote his work in dialogue form and in French.) Galileo's famous trial and condemnation at the hands of the Catholic Inquisition, the result of his miscalculated daring, is a dramatic story of a world-historical confrontation that merits close attention, although it cannot be covered here. Suffice it to say that it gained unprecedented attention, both good and bad, for the new astronomy, which was finally recognized and experienced as the great shock to human complacency and pride that it was—a shock as monumental in its day as those delivered by Darwin and Freud centuries later. Together these three revolutions, in cosmology, in biology, and in psychology, shattered forever all comfortable and facile assumptions about the purpose of human existence.

Galileo's sentencing for "teaching, holding, and defending" Copernicanism, and his famous or infamous recantation, understandably inhibited others who were considering publishing on the subjects of physics and astronomy, or, as they were called at the time, "natural philosophy." One such person was René Descartes, a Catholic Frenchman whose work was in some ways much more innovative and menacing to ancient and Christian authority than Galileo's. Descartes's *Discourse on Method,* which he finally published in 1637, is of revolutionary significance for the history and philosophy of science, as is his even longer-delayed *Principles of Philosophy* (1644). Together they challenged all received opinion, championed the methodical doubting of everything previously believed, and put forth the first complete physical system of the universe since Aristotle. As Descartes's influence on Fontenelle would be enormous, we should look a bit more closely at his ideas.

Descartes believed that to achieve certainty, the human mind must first unload itself of all tradition, of all preconceived ideas, and put them through rigorous testing and the closest scrutiny. This thoroughgoing willingness to doubt distinguished Descartes as one of the world's most daring thinkers, and Fontenelle admired his independence, his courage in the face of vested authority, his irreverence toward the intellectual heritage. He liked his method, his habit of mind, his philosophical orientation far more than his results, for the universal system Descartes arrived at seemed to Fontenelle provisional, subject itself to the same questioning and criticism. Therefore Fontenelle rejected Descartes's ontological proof of God's existence, his doctrine that a few ideas were innate and thus exempt from doubt, most of his metaphysics, and his mind/body dualism. Fontenelle was in fact more like Descartes's contemporary, Francis Bacon, whose scientific method was empirical, subjecting all reason to experimental verification by the senses. But one aspect of Descartes's physics appealed to Fontenelle tremendously, and he was to remain faithful to this theory during his entire long life, despite its being almost immediately discredited by Newton. This was Descartes's theory of vortices, or whirlpools of particles, always in motion, always in contact with each other. In this totally mechanical view of the universe there were no voids, no empty spaces. Instead, atoms of matter continually hit each other, setting up chain reactions of swirling movement that caught up big and small bodies alike, and that spun each planet in its vortex. This theory—unlike Aristotle's, which treated terrestrial and celestial movement separately—assumed the essential similarity of laws of motion for the entire universe, for minute objects as well as for celestial bodies, as they were all in contact through their touching, mutually propelling vortices. Fontenelle found this theory elegant, based as it was on the conviction that nature was uniform and mechanically simple. The theory also seemed to explain what kept the planets in orbit, now that Tycho's observations had "shattered" the crystalline spheres. Descartes's view seemed to Fontenelle far more logical and satisfying than Newton's rival notion of "attraction." Newton's theory of action-at-a-distance, of bodies influencing each other through forces operating across empty space, smacked of the occult, of the strange, mysterious superstitions Fontenelle was determined to combat. It was Descartes's theory of vortices, as we will see, that formed the basic physical explanation of planetary movement in the *Entretiens,* as did Descartes's related beliefs that the universe had no limit, that it was probably not created solely for humankind, that the Earth was materially like the Moon and other planets, and that the stars were made of the same stuff as our Sun.

Now while Fontenelle's *Entretiens* became far better known than any other book for the layperson on the subject of the plurality of worlds, there had been others. Kepler, in his *Somnium* (1634) or astronomical dream, had toyed with the notion of other planets being like Earth, but his was still a very anthropocentric view, in which our Sun was the brightest, our planet the best, our species the noblest. Galileo, who never mentioned his unfortunate countryman, Giordano Bruno, seems nevertheless to have been sobered by the latter's martyrdom, and was uncharacteristically quiet on the possibility of inhabited worlds, saying nothing explicit about the obvious implications of his discoveries for extraterrestrial life. But a young Protestant clergyman in England, John Wilkins, wrote his *Discovery of a World on the Moon* in 1638, in which he argued that the possibility of lunar inhabitants contradicted neither reason nor faith. The work was translated into French and published in Fontenelle's hometown of Rouen in 1655, where it quite probably became known to him as he was growing up. Wilkins's argument that pluralism was not blasphemous, however, probably did relatively little to reassure writers in non-Protestant countries of the safety of the subject. Still, there were free-thinkers even in Catholic France, *libertins* determined to play with these ideas in fanciful disguise. Pierre Borel in 1657 published his *Discours nouveau prouvant la pluralité des mondes.* Cyrano de Bergerac, whose literary merits were made legendary in Rostand's romantic play, gave free reign in 1657 and 1662 to his scientific and technological imagination as he explored hypothetical worlds on the Moon and Sun. The most daring, however, was yet to come. None of these authors had argued for a plurality of solar systems as Fontenelle was soon to do, developing to its logical conclusion Descartes's notion that each of the stars is a sun like ours.

By the time Fontenelle took up this subject, then, the ground had already been broken somewhat, and new astronomical theories were becoming the subject of both debate and entertainment. Still, Copernican cosmology was not universally accepted by any means and was still grossly misunderstood, as evidenced by the reaction to the fiery comet of 1680, much larger and more dramatic than that of 1682 (later to be named after Edmund Halley, the first astronomer to realize its periodicity and to predict its return). This celestial visitor of 1680 caused considerable panic. It was seen by many as an ominous portent of impending doom and the reaction to it was only slightly calmed by the sophisticated astronomical reading matter available. Fontenelle, no doubt surprised and amused by the irony that a comet could still cause extreme anxiety even when the scientific theories on such subjects were supposedly in vogue, wrote a comedy, *La comète* (1681), in which he tried to explain away all worries about it; he tried, according to the French formula, to both "amuse and instruct." Newspapers advertised that now going to the theatre could cure the fear of comets. With this play, Fontenelle first embraced the subject of cosmology and showed his taste and talent for the graceful exposition of scientific material. Although the *Entretiens,* which features a long section on comets, did not appear until five years later, it is plausible that during that time the author began seriously to contemplate and construct the role he would play in winning general acceptance for the new cosmology and dispelling superstitions and outdated ideas

Before going more deeply into the *Entretiens,* Fontenelle's most celebrated, successful, and popular work, it will be helpful to explore a bit more closely his life and some of his other writings against the background of the France of Louis XIV, the so-called *Grand Siècle.*

Fontenelle was born in 1657 in Rouen, a city in provincial Normandy, an area with considerable Protestant roots. This, despite his education at the hands of the Jesuits, would make him an active seeker of religious toleration. His father, a lawyer, wished his son to follow in his profession, but after pleading—and losing—one case, Fontenelle abandoned the law to pursue studies in philosophy and literature. He was a voracious reader and by age fifteen had competed successfully for several literary prizes. His maternal uncles were the famous Corneille brothers. As a teenager he made frequent trips to visit them in Paris, where they introduced him to the world of the theatre, in which Pierre Corneille was widely regarded as the greatest writer of tragedies since Aeschylus, and to the world of the new periodical press, where Thomas Corneille was active on the editorial board of one of the first Parisian newspapers, the *Mercure galant.* This was primarily a literary paper filled with *pièces fugitives* (short prose and poetry), book reviews, and theatre criticism. It targeted an elite, cultured audience. Not surprisingly, Fontenelle's first literary ventures were in the fields of drama and journalism. Though he was not wildly successful in those areas—he even learned the bitter message of the power of the press when his plays were panned in a rival newspaper!—he was becoming known in fashionable Parisian cultural circles as an intelligent *galant,* a young man of learning, wit, and charm. Through his uncles he came to know well many writers, both male and female. He was a particular favorite among the *précieuses,* the hostesses of the salons, informal gatherings in private homes presided over by influential women who could make or break careers, and around whom savants and men of letters flocked. Here Fontenelle mingled with the intellectual stars of the capital, watching, hearing and absorbing, gently challenging, polishing, and refining the discussions. His company was sought after, and numerous salon hostesses, fiercely competitive as a rule, acquiesced to sharing this popular man of the world and putting up with his divided loyalties. It is, I believe, highly significant that in addition to his friendships with female writers, he received this kind of welcome and valorization in the salon, a forum created by women. It was through this female-sponsored institution that he was able to glean a sense of what was intellectually à la mode, a sense of his own strengths as a conversationalist, listener, observer, and interpreter. Not accidentally, he made a woman the eager, enthusiastic, and gracious student in his *Entretiens*. Why should he not acknowledge his debt and immortalize his gratitude to the women who helped shape his career.

The 1680s were very productive years for Fontenelle, who was helped at all times by his female supporters and by the highly effective publicity instrument that was the *Mercure galant*. This paper was read increasingly by women, and in taking them seriously it did much to create a new market, later to be targeted by an explicitly feminine press. We have already seen that Fontenelle wrote *La comète* in 1681. Other plays followed. In 1683 he wrote *Nouveaux dialogues des morts,* in which were brought together for conversation mythological figures, important thinkers, and political actors from different ages. For reasons which should by now be clear, many of the characters were women—poets, goddesses, queens. Already in this early work Fontenelle attacked dogmatic philosophical systems and spoke of the difficulty of discovering truth; he projected a healthy preservative form of skepticism and attacked gullibility in all its forms. Here Fontenelle's fancy, as he put it, was that living people say plenty of useless things, but the dead have more experience, leisure, and time to think, and can perhaps illuminate certain issues for us.

In 1685 Pierre Bayle, the Huguenot journalist who fled France for Rotterdam and published in exile his *Nouvelles de la république des lettres,* printed Fontenelle's *Mémoire sur le nombre neuf,* showing that even in his twenties he was already taking an interest in mathematics as part of his province. In 1686, along with the *Entretiens,* the *Histoire des oracles* and the *Relation curieuse de l'île de Bornéo* were written. The second was a thinly disguised protest against Louis XIV's revocation of the Edict of Nantes which withdrew toleration of Protestants in France, forcing them to flee in enormous numbers, and which would result later in France's political isolation and economic decline. The *Histoire des oracles* was an extraordinary work, almost a comparative history of religions, in which Fontenelle collected different myths and legends and analyzed them to show various stages in the development of humanity's understanding of nature. He argued that people had, since earliest times, been capable of reason, but that they needed to be set free from their belief in marvels and magic, disengaged from traditional superstitions and false teachings. Of course Fontenelle's mockery of supernatural explanations, his critical approach to oracles and prophesies, cast doubt upon Christian miracles as well. That he was not punished for the controversial opinions expressed in these works can largely be explained by his mastery of a tone of *insouciance* which lent a flip, evasive quality to his writings. Though he propagated extremely unorthodox views, he was never heavy-handed or dogmatic.

Fontenelle's *Digression sur les anciens et les modernes* was published two years after the *Entretiens* in 1688. The Quarrel of the Ancients and the Moderns pitted traditionalists who approved of absolute monarchy and thought the Golden Age was in the past—the dramatist Racine, Boileau, La Bruyère, La Fontaine—against such "beaux esprits" as Fontenelle and other admirers of Corneille, Charles Perrault, and the *Mercure galant* staff, who were open to novelty, who believed that political power should serve the whole nation, and who cherished their independence. In taking the side of the Moderns, Fontenelle explained that while ancient literature might be as great as ours, the sciences surely had advanced steadily since days of old, and dramatically in recent years. With a perspective and vision quite astonishing for one so close, Fontenelle even identified the Scientific Revolution (though he did not label it as such), the immense leap taken in understanding the natural world since the mid-sixteenth century. Science, he argued, emancipated humanity from ignorance and prejudice, made us less the slaves of our passions. The scientist's allegiance to knowledge was far more admirable than the politician's pursuit of power. Though folly and vanity might persist through all ages, the worthy study of nature would only enhance the human experience. Fontenelle hoped such advance might continue, unfettered by wars, indifferent governments, religious prejudice, or fanaticism.

The year 1691 saw Fontenelle's reception at the Académie Française, an honor most writers considered the pinnacle of their careers. But this author, who seemed almost to sense that he had more than another half century of intellectual activity in front of him, set his sights ahead and began now actively to cultivate the Académie des Sciences, many of whose members were already friends and acquaintances. In 1697 he was named its perpetual secretary, taking over this function from the aged Du Hamel, a fellow Normand who had dutifully been writing the history of the Academy in Latin. This work was uninspired and inaccessible to most readers. It was undoubtedly the huge success of Fontenelle's *Entretiens*, his ability to create an appetite for science, that brought him to mind for the secretary's post, which the Academy hoped he would exploit as their propagandist. He did not disappoint them. He immediately recognized that the doings of the Academy and of its many distinguished members would have to be written about in French to reach a wide public and to create in the outside world the proper appreciation for this institution. He also began the tradition of *éloges*, brief biographies of each recently deceased academician, filled with subtle psychological observations, clear and elegant explanations and evaluations of each man's work, and an overarching image of scientists as a kind of secular sainthood in disinterested pursuit of knowledge. Scientists showed a seriousness of purpose, a respect for discipline, a determination to find answers, which were their own reward. In the *éloges*, which had shed the playful tone of the *Entretiens* but were still eminently readable, the investigation of nature was described by Fontenelle as a solemn duty, but also an immense pleasure. The contemplation of nature's wonders elevated the soul. Fontenelle realized that though scientific research could yield fruit as well as light—it could have considerable practical utility—it would be stifled by too much emphasis on applications, and therefore pure investigations must always continue to be encouraged. He saw his *éloges* not only as a way to excite the public about unsung scientific heroes but also as a reminder to scientists that a bright though untrained audience awaited news of their work and should be treated with respect. The *éloges* covered everything from architectural engineering through biology and astronomy to political arithmetic. Indeed, Fontenelle in his *éloges* remained ever fresh, always awed by the wonder of unraveling nature's riddles, and continually able to communicate that sense of exhilaration. Daring scientists, his audience learned, trespassed where no human had gone before. In discussing the astronomer Cassini, for example, who like Galileo went blind toward the end of his life, Fontenelle mused that "these two great men made so many discoveries in the sky that they resemble Tiresias, who lost his sight for having seen some secrets of the gods."

Fontenelle lived one month short of one hundred years and continued to write *éloges* and other works almost until his death in 1757. He died without suffering, telling his doctor at the end that he felt simply "a difficulty in being" [une difficulté d'être]. He achieved and maintained celebrity status, and knew most of the influential people of his time. Yet he always cherished his independence. His friendship with the Régent, Philippe d'Orléans, who ruled during Louis XV's minority and who actually gave Fontenelle an apartment in the beautiful Palais Royal, never in any way compromised his free spirit. He knew how to cultivate his reputation, how to gain prestige and influence, in short how to survive in France. Though he expressed views every bit as bold as Pierre Bayle's, he was not exiled because he developed gentler strategies to fight the fight safely from inside. Fontenelle liked calm and comfort and disliked aggressive polemics or anything upsetting. Though his curiosity spanned all fields and kept him in a state of perpetual intellectual thirst, he relished the serenity and satisfaction of learned contemplation, the thinking through and figuring out of the many problems he posed to himself, first in the privacy of his own mind, then for his adoring public. Nor did it hurt that he was fast friends with the Marquis d'Argenson, keeper of the seals and chief of police, who more than once saved Fontenelle from persecution and prosecution for his bold, unorthodox ideas. Many an author in this period was harassed, imprisoned, or forced to flee France with authorities in hot pursuit. Many had their books censored, publicly condemned and burned. During periods of witch-hunting, when the government issued *lettres de cachet* for the arrest (without trial or recourse) of subversive authors, Fontenelle enjoyed a kind of unofficial immunity thanks to d'Argenson. Fontenelle's inimitable style, his ability to treat all his subjects so pleasingly, so easily, so elegantly, almost affectionately, and to put forward his views, however iconoclastic, as proposals, conjectures, suggestions—this too helped him stay safe, active, and able to continue publishing. As Montesquieu once said admiringly of Fontenelle, one can say many important and serious things while joking.

It is always said that Fontenelle was a great popularizer of science, a superb mediator, but this must be understood correctly. While granting his matchless talent as a communicator and interpreter, the modern reader must not conceive Fontenelle as a bridge between two cultures, one scientific and the other humanistic. Nor should we fall into the trap of picturing experts producing knowledge and Fontenelle diluting it for popular consumption. Rather, the author of the *Entretiens* gives us an invaluable insight into the early modern world, when science was still in its adolescence, still searching for its purpose and its self-image, still seeking a public to understand it, make it welcome, foster and even guide it. C. P. Snow's "two cultures" had not yet polarized the terrain of ideas. Scientists were not yet professional specialists in the sense they are today, separated from the layperson by sophisticated technical jargon. The *Entretiens* provides important clues, and we must be sensitive to them. It would be unfortunate to miss the openness of the exchange taking place in Fontenelle's dialogue, the reciprocity of the talk, the flow of the give and take, the common meanings of the language. We have here a delightfully balanced piece of writing, full of analogies that blend with grace the literary and scientific, romantic and serious, playful and profound. The *Entretiens* was written at a time when the pursuit of knowledge still enjoyed great unity, and fields had not yet separated to lose touch with each other. Fontenelle's talents spanned ideas in all their manifestations. He could listen to questions from and share his responses with a wide, varied audience. The notions he sought to communicate were difficult, but it was axiomatic that they were accessible to anyone who bothered to follow along. Of course, in these dialogues, a teacher speaks to a student, yet he needs the student as much as the student needs him. Acceptance, a friendly atmosphere, and society's value and esteem were necessary not only for science's reception and healthy propagation but also for its self-definition. Fontenelle wrote a conversation, not a lecture, in which both interlocutors partook of a common culture, a broad, all-encompassing curiosity that made just about any topic fair game.

Indeed, as we have seen, in a writing career that lasted nearly a century, Fontenelle did touch upon nearly every topic. In his breadth he may have been the last Renaissance man, but he was also the first of the *philosophes* ushering in the new age of the Enlightenment. He represents a transition, a link, between an age steeped in faith, tradition, and reverence to past authority, and an age characterized by a secular spirit, independence, and openness to the future. Fontenelle was no facile optimist, but his conviction that the accumulation of knowledge had enhanced and enriched humanity inspired the eighteenth-century belief in progress as expressed in the great *Encyclopédie* and as epitomized in the writings of Condorcet.

With this background we are ready to look more closely at the *Entretiens* itself, one of the most important works of its time and a beloved, immortal classic. It is a literary masterpiece. Fontenelle's training, we must not forget, was in philosophy and belles-lettres. Though profoundly influenced by and attracted to the new science, he could trace his skepticism back even further to humanistic roots, to the writings of Lucretius, Machiavelli, and Montaigne. Thanks to such authors he realized early the relativity of knowledge, the possibility and richness of numerous points of view on any given issue, and the importance of high style, clarity, precision, rhetorical grace, and narrative strategies in getting a multiplicity of ideas and meanings across. In his *Preface,* Fontenelle explicitly stressed his debt to literature by likening this work to a romance or novel, in particular to the popular *La Princesse de Clèves* by his friend Mme de Lafayette. Anyone who could figure out a plot and keep characters straight could as easily follow him on his extraordinary cosmic voyage. His genius for inventing apt similies and analogies (rolling balls, sailing ships, mulberry leaves), for explaining natural philosophy in terms of everyday thoughts and experiences, for recognizing and welcoming even the fictional dimension of all scientific speculation, allowed him to ease his reader into difficult, sophisticated material. The finesse and dexterity of his writing thus served a democratizing function among the literate. While we must not get carried away imagining everyone reading this book—literacy rates were low in seventeenth-century France and the vast majority of the population could not read—still Fontenelle spread the habit of scientific thought and methodical doubt to the entire *reading* public. As the Duc de Nivernais said, Fontenelle had the power and skill "to make reason a common thing, to introduce and establish it in all genres and in all minds."

Fontenelle could engender excitement effortlessly, it seemed. His topic, of course, had a thrilling, timeless fascination. The author was only twenty-nine when the *Entretiens* appeared, and it had a youthful, spontaneous, even reckless quality about it that immediately created a sensation. Spinning a tale of infinite space, wondrous and strange inhabitants on other planets, in other galaxies, and even on comets, could hardly fail to captivate. The press, especially the loyal *Mercure galant*, cooperated by giving an advance notice of the work that made it sound exceptionally inviting and provocative. The friendly, flirtatious atmosphere of Fontenelle's dialogue made it more naturally conversational. This chat between a philosopher and a Marquise, as they strolled in a beautiful garden looking at the night sky, was even more attractive to the reader than the comparatively formal dialogues of Plato and Galileo, though these too had been very engaging. But Fontenelle had struck on an extremely inventive pedagogical technique, coaxing the reader to participate by identifying either with the smart though untrained student or her knowledgeable, versatile teacher.

The structure of the work merits some comment, for it belies the apparent effortlessness of the exposition. Fontenelle tells us in his *Preface* that he will never be dry, but that he will digress and embellish more at the beginning to break the reader in. He pulls off the work with great élan and panache, but he has done his homework, and has given long hard thought to how best to present his material. The work is divided into five parts, or "evenings," during which the couple behold the skies. The first part sets forth the system of Copernicus as that most likely to be correct, but not without exploring the older alternative views. The second and third discuss the Moon and the possibility of travel to it, an area already explored as we saw in several earlier imaginary lunar voyages by Wilkins, Borel, and Cyrano. Thus the first three "evenings" broach subjects that might be somewhat familiar to readers in the know already. Only then, after easing the reader into it, does Fontenelle allow himself to cover totally new ground. The fourth part deals with Descartes's difficult physics of vortices as an explanation for all planetary motion. And the fifth takes the radical plunge into discussing the fixed stars as suns, around which an infinity of habitable planets probably revolve. The Milky Way is described as a "cluster of worlds." Suddenly the universe becomes infinite, teeming with bizarre but intelligent life everywhere. And the reader, lulled by the gradual seduction of earlier, more familiar suggestions, does not really experience this news as a shock. Fontenelle had said early on in the *Entretiens* that truth should be pleasing. He had a sense of the aesthetics, the beauty of simple conclusions, and here he succeeded in putting forth astonishing ideas as if they were entirely natural. The author was a master of gamesmanship. Philosophy, he said, was based on curiosity and poor eyesight. We want to know more than we can see. So together, we do some educated guesswork based on judicious observation and clear thinking, and if we are careful, respecting both the economy and the fertility of nature—that she is uniform in her laws but varied in her manifestations—then we will ultimately arrive at conjectures that ring true.

Not only structurally, but in more subtle ways, Fontenelle lures his reader into a frame of mind ready to brave the new world he is presenting. At the outset the philosopher flatters and teases the Marquise, and it is she who repeatedly urges him to drop all the frills and explain the facts. He is not so easily persuaded to abandon the colorful moral digressions, and introduces the notion that the Earth is not central with a homily on human vanity. Cloaking his discussion in flowery terms, he explains that Copernicus wrested Earth from her proud posturing, hurtled her into the skies, and, as punishment for her conceit at thinking she was the purpose for which all nature was created, gave her many movements and much extra work to do. Some recent feminist scholars have seen a misogynistic strain in this treatment of Mother Earth, and perhaps the Marquise herself senses it. As she continues to protest the philosopher's innuendoes and off-color jokes, he slips in the notion that nature is quite indifferent to humanity, that we must realize ours is only one of many perspectives, that we must be willing to play with them all rather than remain fixated on our own importance. The philosopher, who had earlier commented on his pupil's ability to "arrange things in her mind, without confusion," compliments her at the end of this first session on her "lively and prompt discernment." By the second night he realizes a review is unnecessary, that his student is ready to go on to new material. She catches on so fast, in fact, that he says he would not wish to be reproached for belaboring points. Thus he encourages the reader to keep up a healthy pace and see, as does his pupil, that there is really "no mystery" to his explanations, though foolish superstitions still persist among those who do not bother to think. Nevertheless at the end of the second evening, he has pressed things too far. The Marquise uses her healthy skepticism on his argument, and things do not end as placidly, perhaps a reminder to readers and teachers alike that learning is not a linear progression, that the rhythms of the mind's readiness and resistance need to be respected.

By the third evening, he retracts his bold assertion that the Moon is inhabited, but twenty-four hours have passed and by now the Marquise has had time to think about the possibility, and has grown accustomed to the idea. She even likes it. She says now that she finds it difficult, almost impossible, to suspend judgment on something like that, to be aloof or indifferent to these wonders her teacher describes, thus showing how impressionable students are, how eager, whatever the subject, to have solutions to believe in. Together they muse on what the world would look like from the Moon, and this whets her appetite to "travel" on. She wants to render their speculations visually concrete, to draw pictures of the various inhabitants of other worlds. On the fourth evening, however, she complains about the frustrating limits of her own imagination. Even in dreams she can only come up with variations on human themes, and seems incapable of conjuring up totally different forms of life. In this fourth part the philosopher makes the incredibly bold remark that the planets are where they are because of "chance alone" [le seul hasard de la situation] at the beginning of the world. Earth *could* have been a moon of Jupiter if chance had caught us in its vortex. Does this perhaps hint at there being no creator, or at least no grand design? Elsewhere the philosopher had said that inhabitants of other planets were not sons of Adam, implying that they were not part of the Christian drama of fall and redemption. It is interesting to contemplate just how much Fontenelle's own views are represented by the philosopher, and just how far he meant readers to go with this suggestion of ultimate skepticism. At least one of his translators, while not labeling him an atheist, was convinced he was a "pagan."

The Marquise now expresses pleasure at the idea that Jupiter's astronomers might be eager to learn about us. This possibility of mutual curiosity fascinates her. To counter the philosopher's half-hearted, scattered, yet persistent suggestion that indifference, play, and chance might be the ways of nature, the Marquise now argues, as they discuss the rings of Saturn and the great reflected light these rings must surely provide, that nature is a caring, almost maternal guardian who keeps the needs of her creatures in mind. The discussion of the characteristics of the inhabitants of Earth, undertaken now from a comparative cosmic perspective, is an amusing but sobering social satire.

By the fifth evening, when the philosopher presses on to discuss the myriad stars as suns, the Marquise has a fleeting moment of alarm. The

enormity of the universe suddenly frightens and humbles her, as it re-
duces humanity almost to insignificance. But she recovers quickly, and
thrills to the possibility that the inhabitants of comets, which slice
through different vortices, would get to see the planets around many
different suns and thus have an especially rich and varied experience.
Toward the end the Marquise mourns the fact that, according to her
teacher, some suns go out. This notion of the expiration or extinguish-
ing of heavenly lights upsets her, but the philosopher takes the opportunity to introduce the changeability of the universe, the idea that
things come and go, live and die, that new worlds are being created as
others fade away, that the cosmic voyager must travel in time as well
as space to truly understand.

The edition of the *Entretiens* translated here is Fontenelle's first, that
of 1686. One year later the work was placed on the Catholic index of
prohibited books, but this did not deter the author from publishing a
new edition with a sixth "evening" added. This was basically a summary
of the major points he had already made in the work, but one which
brought to bear more forceful evidence and abandoned the argument
for chance. He stressed the similarity in physical composition of the
Earth and planets, strengthening the likelihood that the planets are inhabited. He underscored the difficulty in figuring out why the other
planets were created, if not to house living creatures. In connection
with this, he stressed the principle of plenitude, made popular by Leib-
niz, that nature is fecund, magnificent and full, that none of it goes to
waste, or is created in vain. This perspective was probably further inspired by the discoveries Leeuwenhoek made with his microscope in
the 1670s of tiny worlds filled with infinitesimal "animalcules" never
before seen. Great orbs, like minute drops of water, must indeed be
populated too. Just because the naked eye failed to detect things did
not mean they did not exist, and Fontenelle argued that the limitation
of our senses should not paralyze our scientific imagination. He put
forth an interesting new argument, no doubt influenced by Bayle's critical writings on history, that historical facts were no more certain than
cosmological ones. Our conviction, for example, that Alexander the
Great existed, is based on no firmer evidence than these astronomical
verities. There were, then, he summed up, many sound reasons for believing his conjectures, and hardly any for rejecting them. Perhaps he
felt that the ending of the fifth evening, by leaving things up in the air

and giving the Marquise the choice of ignoring all she had learned, had made the new system seem optional to the reader as well. The Marquise had even commented that he would never a martyr make, playing as he did with ideas but failing to commit himself to one side or the other. While acknowledging once again that it was neither chic nor safe to insist on something, Fontenelle came back in this last added evening to urge more persuasively the view to which he subscribed. And the Marquise ended by demanding she be treated henceforth not as a novice but as a *docteur,* or learned person.

Fontenelle continued over many decades to update and correct new editions of the *Entretiens,* most notably in 1708 and 1742, based on the newest astronomical data provided by his colleagues and friends in the Academy of Sciences. In this sense he kept the work alive, preserving the spontaneity and exuberance of its first appearance on the literary scene, recapturing its freshness. He changed the size of Venus several times in response to new observations, incorporated Kepler's theory of elliptical orbits which Newton had meanwhile made better known, and even altered literary and political references to keep the work current and timely. During his lifetime his ever-renewed *Entretiens* inspired a new genre, the hundreds of utopian novels and imaginary voyages that proliferated throughout Europe but especially in France during the eighteenth century. These pioneering works of science fiction, with their visions of alternative societies and futures, experienced a tremendous vogue.

What sort of audience did Fontenelle have in mind? To what sociocultural milieu did he address this work, and what motivated him? One of his biographers has suggested that he had a fine nose for what was fashionable, and knew the *Entretiens* would be a financial success that would catapult him to fame and fortune. Others have found more lofty motives in Fontenelle's determination to appeal to a wider reading public as arbiter of thought in order to share his relativistic world view. But while he meant to enlighten the literate elite, he was no democrat, and had no interest in converting the masses. The study of nature was healthy, even necessary, for the leisured classes; they should all be "spectators of the world." This would not result in worship or love for a creator—Fontenelle did not think that necessary—but rather in respect and admiration for the wonder of it all, and in a healthy perspective balanced somewhere between humility and pride. For the lower classes, however, he seemed to hold little hope. Fontenelle had no tolerance for people "too tender in religious matters." He maintained an audaciously anti-clerical stance in all his writings and did not address the "ignorant masses" whom he felt would never transcend their historical limitations. The *Histoire des oracles* had portrayed prophets as masters of trickery and priests as deceitful, power-hungry frauds who prey on the gullibility of their flock to achieve power. The duped, it seemed, were as much to blame as the charlatans. In the *Entretiens* Fontenelle made unflattering remarks even about popes. He toyed with the possible role of chance in the world. His skepticism, his general unbelieving attitude, made religion of any kind relatively unimportant for him, and distanced him from those dependent on faith, as were most commoners. It was folly, he tried to show in the *Entretiens,* to believe that the universe was a private affair between humanity and God. He served up to his sophisticated or at least culturally aware readers, as delicately and gently as possible, the fact of their relative cosmic insignificance. Presenting them—and us—with this unsettling paradox, he assumed, would encourage active, intelligent debate among those who could exercise their reason in order to discover truth. Fontenelle spoke only to a public he considered worthy of him.

That women were included in Fontenelle's invitation to ponder and resolve the meaning of existence was extraordinary for his day. This, as much as anything else, makes the *Entretiens* an exceptional and enduring work. Misogyny was rampant in seventeenth-century France—in most of Europe for that matter—and while the *question de la femme* had begun to be actively debated, with a few partisans of women even arguing provocatively for their superiority, the majority of writers treated the female as a subhuman species. The development of the salons and the growing influence of women as readers and as theatre-goers seemed menacing to men who sought to maintain their hegemony as arbiters of cultural taste. Attempts on the part of women to educate themselves were experienced by most male intellectuals as a threat to their jurisdiction over the province of scholarship; such women were mercilessly ridiculed. Molière's famous comedy, *Les femmes savantes,* mocked the *précieuses* for seeking to better their understanding, for involving themselves in anything other than trivial, mindless pursuits. This play, in which women were damned if they did think and damned if they did not, appeared only fourteen years before Fontenelle's *Entretiens,* and represented quite accurately the prevailing view of intellectually ambitious women at that time.

Fontenelle, though he never wrote explicitly feminist tracts, simply gave women the benefit of the doubt. They deserved his attention. He casually, calmly addressed his remarks to them, as if to say come, follow, all this knowledge can be yours with the same kind of effort that allows you to understand literature. His Marquise is worth considering in some detail. She is charming, sensitive, humorous, quick, though totally unschooled. He uses her in a unique way in the dialogue, not as a person with views opposed to his own—as was the case with Plato and Galileo, and as again would be the case with Diderot a century later—but as a mind ready to be filled, yet quickly developing the capacity to question and criticize, to evaluate and challenge in its own right. Hers is a mind unspoiled by false teaching, and thus all the more promising for proper cultivation. She has an identity; we learn of her social class, her looks, her garden. By the end we can almost predict her reactions. She chooses to spend her time learning astronomy rather than dancing, hunting, or gaming, as do most of her social rank. She gets impatient with the philosopher's gallantries, and in the course of her instruction seems to grow in self-esteem. More than the various tracts on the education of girls, Fontenelle's Marquise did much to justify equal instruction for both sexes. Though the telescope and microscope had by this time become fashionable toys for ladies, this woman seeks to understand the whole cosmic system and craves learning of a deeper sort. Despite her lack of training, she catches on fast. What seems at first like flirtatious naiveté on her part almost immediately develops into genuine curiosity.

Not surprisingly, one of the earliest English translations of the *Entretiens* was done by a woman, Aphra Behn, already famous in her own right as a dramatist, poet, and novelist, the first woman in England to earn a living by her pen. Using the title *A Discovery of New Worlds,* her translation came out in 1688, just two years after the first appearance of the *Entretiens* in France. She explained that she had wanted to write her own work on astronomy, but that, having neither the health nor the leisure to do so, she instead decided to translate a new book that seemed to her quite fine. She commented on Fontenelle's skill in arguing his points, and praised his examples and comparisons as "extraordinary," "just," "natural," and "lofty." Interestingly, she had some objections to the Marquise, whom she found unrealistic, saying things at times silly, at times so profound that only the great sages would understand her. Behn's inability to identify with the aristocratic Marquise in her château may have resulted from her being a middle-class, city-dwelling woman exercising a profession. Or perhaps she considered science somehow still a male province. Behn, for all her accomplishments and reputation, at times adopted a diffident stance, explaining for example that she too agreed with the Copernican system, "as far as a woman's reasoning can go." Was she somehow unready for, or suspicious of, Fontenelle's tacit assumption that a "woman's reasoning" was no different than a man's? This ambivalence on Behn's part— her obvious attraction to this book for its inclusion of women but her hesitance over her sex's trespassing too boldly into the sciences—should remind us not to see the seventeenth century through the prism of modern feminism, but instead to be attuned to the nuances of women's first halting attempts to emerge from centuries of intellectual subordination. Modesty was a necessary strategy for the few female writers of the day. Behn knew that women who wrote pleasingly and agreeably and maintained a deferential attitude would have far more male listeners than their coarse, strident colleagues. There was, in this period, considerable hypocrisy in both directions, critics trying to be indulgent and courteous, and women playing their game. Thus Behn, in the "Dedicatory Epistle" to her translation, asked for special consideration. "If [the translation] is not done with that exactness it merits, I hope your lordship will pardon it in a woman, who is not supposed to be well-versed in the Terms of Philosophy, being but a beginner in the science." Behn went on in her preface to comment that Fontenelle "ascribes all to Nature, and says not a word of God Almighty from the Beginning to the End; so that one would almost take him to be a Pagan." But she then agreed that religion has no place in such a work anyway and ventured to list many inaccuracies and inconsistencies in Scripture. "The design of the Bible was not to instruct in Astronomy, Geometry, or Chronology, but in the Law of God." Anything that sounds scientific in Scripture is allegorical, and can be distorted to "fit the common acceptance or appearances of things to the vulgar." Thus Behn, because her disclaimers liberated her, dealt boldly with the issues raised by Fontenelle's work, even ventured some literary criticism and biblical hermeneutics, and somehow managed to make the whole package acceptable. She was cunning, and her tactics reveal much about the codes deployed by women who wished to get into print.

In England, at least as much as in France, Fontenelle's *Conversations* became a classic for women readers, and his Marquise a model for the "scientific lady." Magazines, books, and lecture series began to be aimed at women. Entrepreneurs were quick to exploit the new female market as buyers of scientific instruments and newspapers. John Dunton's twice-weekly *Athenian Mercury* and its sister publication, *The Ladies Mercury,* addressed primarily to the woman reader, treated scientific material, although still sometimes in a satirical vein, throughout the early 1690s. Soon, though, things got more serious. Papers edited by Richard Steele and Joseph Addison aimed at "the improvement of ladies." The *Guardian,* in 1713, portrayed a memorable scene of a mother and her daughters reading Fontenelle aloud to each other as they made jam. The *Spectator,* another paper, summed up Fontenelle's ideas and encouraged women to learn about nature. Algarotti's *Il newtonianismo per le dame* or *Newton for the Ladies,* dedicated to Fontenelle, spread the taste for scientific research to Italian women. In general throughout Europe in the eighteenth century, women began to involve themselves increasingly in scientific investigation. Where Fontenelle's Marquise had been essentially passive, a beginner, a listener, the scientific ladies of the following century actually did laboratory work, went out observing and collecting, dissected cadavers, got grubby. Some of them even became teachers and editors, taking a more aggressive approach as propagators, not mere recipients, of scientific wisdom. Eliza Haywood and Charlotte Lennox became journalists in England, editors respectively of the *Female Spectator* and the *Lady's Museum,* instructing their subscribers on their original microscopic researches, seeking "artfully to cajole fair readers into seriousness." The Italian Laura Bassi got a doctorate and teaching post in physics at the University of Bologna. In France, Bassi's praises were sung in the first newspaper "par et pour les femmes" the *Journal des Dames.* Another paper edited by a woman, the *Nouveau Magasin Français,* was full of articles on the scientific work of the Academy of Rouen. The Marquise du Châtelet, Voltaire's longtime companion, did numerous physical experiments and was the first person of either sex to translate Newton into French. Today, at the end of the twentieth century, though we no longer feel the patronizing need

XXX INTRODUCTION

to compose separate science texts for female readers, women are still
vastly underrepresented in the sciences, mathematics, technology, and
medicine. That they have developed into a strong and growing presence
in these fields, however, and have the self-respect and courage to strive
for equality here as in other domains, may perhaps in some measure
be traced back to the quiet but steady vote of confidence given them
by Fontenelle.

The *Entretiens,* then, is a work that resonates with meanings for our
own time on many levels; some have been suggested here, many others
wait in the pages that follow to strike different chords in each of us.
But more precious even than its enduring relevance is the window it
provides into an earlier age, that of seventeenth-century French culture.
This work represents the convergence of numerous social assumptions,
stylistic strategies, and intellectual preoccupations of another historical
period, and studying it closely allows us to time-travel backward into
that world. Fontenelle, who journeyed so gracefully through space and
other ages, would wish us *bon voyage.*

Bibliography

Alic, Margaret. *Hypatia's Heritage: A History of Women in Science from Antiquity to the Late Nineteenth Century.* London: Women's Press, 1986.
Biagioli, Mario. "Galileo the Emblem-Maker." *Isis* 81 (in press).
Brinton, Crane, ed. *The Portable Age of Reason Reader.* New York: Viking, 1956.
Burtt, E. A. *The Metaphysical Foundations of Modern Science.* New York: Doubleday Anchor, 1954.
Butterfield, Herbert. *The Origins of Modern Science.* New York: The Free Press, 1957.
Catalogue de l'exposition Fontenelle à la Bibliothèque Nationale. Paris: Bibliothèque Nationale, 1957.
Collingwood, R. G. *The Idea of Nature.* Oxford: The Clarendon Press, 1945.
Crowe, Michael J. *The Extraterrestrial Life Debate 1750–1900.* Cambridge: Cambridge University Press, 1986.
Delorme, Suzanne. "Contribution à la bibliographie de Fontenelle." *Revue d'histoire des sciences* 10, no. 4 (1957): 300–309.
———. "Fontenelle." In *Dictionary of Scientific Biography,* edited by C. C. Gillispie, vol. 5: 57–63. New York: Scribner, 1972.
Dick, Steven J. *Plurality of Worlds: The Origins of the Extraterrestrial Life*

Debate from Democritus to Kant. Cambridge: Cambridge University Press, 1982.

Drake, Stillman, ed. *Discoveries and Opinions of Galileo.* Garden City, N.Y.: Doubleday, 1957.

Eurich, Nell. *Science in Utopia, A Mighty Design.* Cambridge, Mass.: Harvard University Press, 1967.

Gelbart, Nina Rattner. *Feminine and Opposition Journalism in Old Regime France: Le Journal des Dames.* Berkeley, Los Angeles, Oxford: University of California Press, 1987.

———. "Organicism and the Future of Scientific Utopia." In *Approaches to Organic Form,* edited by F. Burwick, 49–70. Dordrecht: Reidel, 1987.

———. "Science in French Enlightenment Utopias." *Proceedings of the Western Society for French History* 6 (1979): 120–129.

Glotz, Marguerite, and Madeleine Maire. *Salons du 18e siècle.* Paris: Nouvelles éditions latines, 1949.

Hahn, Roger. *The Anatomy of a Scientific Institution: The Paris Academy of Sciences. 1666–1803.* Berkeley, Los Angeles, Oxford: University of California Press, 1971.

Hall, A. R. *The Revolution in Science 1500–1750.* London: Longmans, 1983.

Hall, Marie Boas. *The Scientific Renaissance 1450–1630.* New York: Harper and Row, 1966.

Kearns, Edward John. *Ideas in Seventeenth-Century France.* Manchester: Manchester University Press, 1979.

Koestler, Arthur. *The Sleepwalkers, A History of Man's Changing Vision of the Universe.* New York: Macmillan Co., 1968.

Koyré, Alexander. *From the Closed World to the Infinite Universe.* Baltimore: Johns Hopkins University Press, 1957.

Kuhn, Thomas S. *The Copernican Revolution.* Cambridge, Mass.: Harvard University Press, 1957.

Lenoble, Robert. *Mersenne; ou, La naissance du mécanisme.* Paris: J. Vrin, 1943.

Lougee, Carolyn C. *Le Paradis des Femmes: Women, Salons and Social Stratification in Seventeenth-Century France.* Princeton: Princeton University Press, 1976.

Lough, John. *Introduction to Seventeenth-Century France.* London: Longmans, 1969.

Lovejoy, Arthur O. *The Great Chain of Being.* Cambridge, Mass.: Harvard University Press, 1970.

Maigron, Louis. *Fontenelle: L'homme, l'oeuvre, l'influence.* Geneva: Slatkine Reprints, 1970.

Marsak, Leonard. *Bernard de Fontenelle: The Idea of Science in the French Enlightenment. Transactions of the American Philosophical Society,* n.s. 49, pt. 7, 1959.

Merchant, Carolyn. *The Death of Nature: Women, Ecology and the Scientific Revolution.* New York: Harper and Row, 1980.

Meyer, Gerald Dennis. *The Scientific Lady in England 1650–1760*. Berkeley: University of California Press, 1955.

Nicolson, Marjorie Hope. *Science and Imagination*. Ithaca: Great Seal Books, 1962.

————. *Voyages to the Moon*. New York: Macmillan Co., 1948.

Niderst, Alain. *Fontenelle à la recherche de lui-même 1657–1702*. Paris: A.-G. Nizet, 1972.

Paul, Charles. *Science and Immortality: The Eloges of the Paris Academy of Sciences 1699–1791*. Berkeley, Los Angeles, Oxford: University of California Press, 1980.

Picard, Roger. *Les salons littéraires et la société française 1610–1789*. New York: Brentanos, 1943.

Popkin, Richard H. *The History of Scepticism from Erasmus to Descartes*. Assen: Van Gorcum, 1964.

Redondi, Pietro. *Galileo Heretic*. Translated by Raymond Rosenthal. Princeton: Princeton University Press, 1987.

Rendall, Steven F. "Fontenelle and His Public." *Modern Language Notes* 86 (1971, pt. 2): 496–508.

Santillana, Giorgio de. *The Crime of Galileo*. Chicago: University of Chicago Press, 1976.

Shea, William R. "Galileo and the Church." In *God and Nature: Historical Essays on the Encounter Between Christianity and Science,* edited by David C. Lindberg and Ronald L. Numbers. Berkeley, Los Angeles, Oxford: University of California Press, 1986.

Spink, J. S. *French Free-Thought from Gassendi to Voltaire*. New York: Greenwood Press, 1969.

Van Helden, Albert. *Measuring the Universe: Cosmic Dimensions from Aristarchus to Halley*. Chicago: University of Chicago Press, 1985.

Westfall, Richard S. *The Construction of Modern Science*. Cambridge: Cambridge University Press, 1971.

Westman, Robert S. "The Copernicans and the Churches." In *God and Nature: Historical Essays on the Encounter Between Christianity and Science,* edited by David C. Lindberg and Ronald L. Numbers. Berkeley, Los Angeles, Oxford: University of California Press, 1986.

Zilsel, Edgar. "The Genesis of the Concept of Scientific Progress." *Journal of the History of Ideas* 6, no. 3 (June 1945): 325–364.

Translator's Preface

The art of flying has only just been born; it will be perfected, and some day we'll go to the Moon.

This statement could easily be taken for an early twentieth-century pronouncement. In fact it is translated literally from the *Entretiens sur la Pluralité des Mondes,* first published by Fontenelle just over three hundred years ago. Admittedly these words are less surprising when read in context, where the narrator is describing for that certain Marquise the efforts of his contemporaries to achieve the wonderful freedom of flight.

A number of different people have found the secret of strapping on wings that hold them up in the air, and making them move, and crossing over rivers or flying from one belfry to another. Certainly it's not been the flight of an eagle, and several times it's cost these fledglings an arm or a leg; but yet these represent only the first planks that were placed in the water, which were the beginning of navigation. . . . Still, little by little, the big ships have come. The art of flying has only just been born; it will be perfected, and some day we'll go to the Moon.

This description of flight is not a unique passage in the *Entretiens.* Time after time it is not the quaintness of Fontenelle's expression which strikes us, but the modernity of his ideas. The narrator sounds almost like an astronaut reminiscing when he says:

Suspended clouds hover irregularly around our globe, and sometimes overshadow one country, sometimes another. Whoever could see the Earth from a distance would often notice changes on its surface, because a great continent covered by clouds would be a dark place, and would become brighter as it was uncovered. One would see spots changing their location, arranging themselves differently, or disappearing all at once.

At another point, like our astronaut but with more poetic fervor, he provides this picture:

I often imagine that I'm suspended in the air, motionless, while the Earth turns under me for twenty-four hours, and that I see passing under my gaze all the different faces: white, black, tawny, and olive complexions, that I see first with hats, then turbans; woolly heads, then shaved heads; here cities with belltowers, there cities with tall spires and crescents; here cities with towers of porcelain, there great countries with nothing but huts; here vast seas, there frightful deserts; in all, the infinite variety that exists on the face of the Earth.

The Marquise, herself gifted with a swift, sharp intelligence, is able to imagine herself at this same vantage point. She adds:

And so through this same place where we are now (I'm not speaking of this garden but this same space that we take up in the air), other people might pass continually who take our place, and at the end of twenty-four hours we return.

The narrator, pleased, answers: "Copernicus couldn't have expressed it better."

All this in 1686! The group of conjectures and the observations they rise from, adroitly dressed in a flirtatious style, inspire a series of delightful shocks of recognition as the modern reader moves through the "education" of Fontenelle's Marquise. Yet the truth is that when this enigmatic literary artist, philosopher, and savant (one who could still assume that nearly all knowledge was open to his scrutiny) wrote the *Entretiens,* he stood only at the beginning of the Enlightenment, on the threshhold of the modern era. The *Entretiens,* as Professor Gelbart has already amply demonstrated, was an attempt to bring together not only the relatively new information accumulating about man and his world, but to treat it with a new method, and to express it in emerging concepts at odds with previous thinking. It is not amiss, however, to stress again that beyond Fontenelle, extending back through the seventeenth century and Renaissance, stood a perception of the universe quite alien to us. Theologically based, its order was usually presented in that grand metaphoric image called the Great Chain of Being, descending from God through the ranks of Heavenly beings, men, animals, plants, inanimate objects, the legions of Hell, to Satan at the farthest remove. In each rank the hierarchy of Heaven was paralleled to a minute degree, and the influence of God was felt providentially throughout. The scope of such a universe could also be visualized, as noted, in Ptolemaic terms as a series of spheres, one enclosed within the next, from the sphere of the Empyreal Heaven inward to the homocentric heart of it all, the Earth. For man, so comfortably placed, the proper activities were to study God's immutable laws.

At the time of writing of the *Entretiens,* Fontenelle was intimately involved in a period of profound change. Yet while skepticism of the Ptolemaic world view grew apace and the seeds of modern science were germinating, no dramatic chasm opened between past and present thought. Like his contemporaries, in the main, Fontenelle attempted to cope with old and new together. He was very much a child of his time.

The salient facts of Fontenelle's life have already been presented but it would be useful to note once again his early literary activities. A Latin epigram appeared in 1670, when he was only thirteen. It was the beginning of a prodigious output of remarkable diversity, not all of which may be positively assigned. However, of those pieces that he acknowledged or actually signed, thirty-seven appeared before first publication of the *Entretiens* in 1686. They ranged from short poems and the *Pastorales* to the series of *Lettres galantes* which appeared in the *Mercure galant*; from a comedy, *La comète* (1681), and a tragedy, *Asphar* (1680 or 1681), to the *Nouveaux dialogues des morts* (1683); from a mock eulogy on a dog to the moving *Eloge de Monsieur Corneille* (1685); from the treatise *Mémoire sur le nombre neuf* (1685) to the various ironic romances, such as *Histoire de mes conquêtes* (1681); and these do not include his collaboration with Thomas Corneille on the libretti of two operas in 1678 and 1679. All this he accomplished before he was twenty-nine and, save for a long visit with his famous uncles in Paris during 1674–75, all in the pleasant surroundings of his native Normandy.

By the latter part of this period he had acquired a degree of fame, or perhaps notoriety, in some quarters. Far more important, however, is the significance of his works' content. These were, of course, formative years in which his attitudes towards genres and intellectual issues were solidifying under the influence of reaction to his writings (not always positive), the ideas and counsel of friends, exchanges with "adversaries," his voracious reading, and of course his mixed reactions to Descartes. But despite the continuing evolution of these attitudes, certain stances acquired clear foundations early on, such as his lifelong nostalgia for a kind of pastoral ideal, personified in various historical or fictional characters, and only slightly less obvious in his treatment of the lives and achievements of his contemporaries in the Académie des Sciences. This nostalgia was not the amorphous sort found in the romances, which he ridiculed, but an opposition to what he considered the avaricious, self-gratifying society of his own day. Other long-held attitudes concerned man's never-changing animal nature, his almost mechanical tendency to fall into error (which had produced many mythologies and which was to be overcome by the development of "positive science"), and a controlled skepticism about the uses and abuses of religions.

Are there seeming paradoxes here? They are surely more apparent than substantial, furnished by the same complexity of personality which made the dialogue a superb instrument for Fontenelle when, in 1683, he wrote the *Nouveaux dialogues des morts*. There his participants often argue so clearly and forcefully that there is no definite winner in a particular dialogue, and it is difficult if not impossible to tell where Fontenelle himself stands. It is a quality of mind much like that which his English contemporaries called Wit: the ability to hold diametrically opposed views simultaneously in one's mind. Certainly Niderst painstakingly demonstrates that there is nothing *fundamentally* contradictory about the above stances, nor about Fontenelle's characteristic cheerfulness almost to the point of optimism throughout his later life. They come from the same sources—Saint-Réal, Huet, Saint-Evremond, Spinoza—and reveal Fontenelle's insistence upon seeking out truth wherever he might find it.[1] The reconciliation may be found in the *Entretiens* itself, where the narrator speaks about the healthy effect of man's recognition of his insignificance, yet favored position, in the universe.

No doubt the *Entretiens* could be viewed, as opposed to the earlier *Dialogues,* merely as a vehicle for the author's predetermined ideas, since several scholars view the Marquise as mainly "an intermediary between the author's representative and the public he addresses."[2] In the *Dialogues* the characters, while in some cases fictionalized to laughable caricatures to suit Fontenelle's ironic purposes, often have depth and acutely rendered human foibles which seem both to rise from and to reinforce the positions they defend. Nor is the Marquise by any means a featureless cut-out; she is appropriately able to raise objections or to make witty and perceptive comments while she absorbs this new knowledge. Moreover, Fontenelle demonstrates that same fine ability to use objective contradiction when at several points the narrator presents alternatives to his own speculations. One of the more obvious is that already noted, in the opening to the Third Evening's conversation, when he tells the Marquise that he has now thought of something that would suggest the Moon is not inhabited after all. Piqued, she replies that he mustn't fob her off with words, and persists in her request that he provide a solid case for repopulating it. Here he protests with a telling admonition: "You should never give more than half your mind to beliefs of this sort, and keep the other half free so that the contrary can be admitted if it's necessary," after which he supplies several conjectures concerning the atmosphere of the Moon and its effect on the kind of inhabitants who might live there. Whimsical as some of these contradictions may be, the suggestion is present that Fontenelle was to some extent writing with an immediacy of doubt, and perhaps with an intent to alleviate that doubt for himself.

The bases of such an open and questioning stance have been traced to well-known Cartesian principles, augmented and adapted to concepts and attitudes of Fontenelle's *libertin* contemporaries (those *"philosophes"* who wished to pursue truth free from the dogma, and often doctrine, of the Church). Like the *libertins,* he would rely on reason rather than faith, and he would seek for natural laws as the causes which produced observed phenomena. In this last, differing from extremist *libertins* who became avowed atheists, he attempted discreetly throughout his career to reconcile general doctrine (as distinct from dogma) and most new investigative precepts, always publicly acknowledging God as Creator, but suggesting that whatever providential influence might be discerned in earthly affairs was impersonal, imparted by divinely created Nature rather than by divine intervention. It takes no stretch of the imagination to assume that Fontenelle and his narrator speak as one when, in the First Evening's conversation, "Descartes and some other moderns" are credited with likening the world to a great machine, and the Marquise says: "Well, I hold it in higher regard . . . now that I know it's like a watch: it's superb that, wonderful as it is, the whole order of Nature is based upon such simple things." Pointedly the narrator replies: "I don't know who's given you such healthy ideas."

Fontenelle took pains to suggest that not all knowledge was the proper goal of men like himself. Let metaphysics remain out of his province; he would content himself with seeking for that knowledge contained in Nature that was useful in the everyday affairs of men. If, after all, the world is essentially mechanical, then there are observable laws by which it, in fact all of Nature, is governed. "Nowadays," says the narrator in the First Evening's conversation, "we believe no longer that a body will move if it's not affected by another body; we don't believe that it will rise or fall except when it has a spring or a counter-weight. Whoever sees Nature as it truly is, sees the backstage of a theatre." These laws apply to all the natural world. In the end, all sciences are subdivisions of one science which is purely (though perhaps not simply) the mathematical inter-relationship of all tangible phenomena. Hence Fontenelle can say wryly in the Fifth Evening, "grant a mathematician the least principle, he'll draw a conclusion from it that you must grant him, and from that conclusion another too, and in spite of yourself he'll lead you so far you'll have trouble believing it."

From that comment he proceeds to an example which suggests, in fact, one of the most important conclusions he promulgated: that of the economy and uniformity of nature. Says his narrator:

You agree that when things seem alike to me in all apparent ways, I can then believe they're equally alike in ways that aren't apparent, if there's nothing to hinder me. From that I've concluded that the Moon is inhabited because it resembles the Earth, the other planets because they resemble the Moon. I find that the fixed stars resemble our Sun; I attribute all it has to them.

He had already made use of this argument in the Third Evening, to make his first major statement on pluralism (a plurality of worlds or, in our terms, inhabited worlds scattered through the universe). Moreover, he had extended it to integrate it with the extant Christian concept of the Great Chain of Being:

It would be very strange that the Earth was as populated as it is, and the other planets weren't at all, for you mustn't think that we see all those who inhabit the Earth; there are as many species of invisible animals as visible.

There follows a vivid, lengthy passage on the incredible world revealed by the marvelous microscope, toward the end of which Fontenelle, through his narrator, returns to the notion of some kind of inhabitants for the Moon and other worlds.

Even in very hard kinds of rock we've found innumerable small worms. . . . Imagine how many of these little worms there may be, and how many years they've subsisted on the mass of a grain of sand. Following this example, even if the Moon were only a mass of rocks, I'd sooner have her gnawed by her inhabitants than not put any there at all.

He has not yet really made the second important conclusion clear, that of the rich diversity of Nature, but in the following discussion the Marquise comments:

My imagination's overwhelmed by the infinite multitude of inhabitants on all these planets, and perplexed by the diversity one must establish among them; for I can see that Nature, since she's an enemy of repetition, will have made them all different.

The narrator then uses the opportunity to make an analogy of human faces, which seem "to have been made on two specific models. . . . What secret must Nature have possessed to vary in so many ways so simple a thing as a face?" He presses the point. "In the universe we're no more than one little family whose faces resemble one another: on another planet is another family whose faces have another cast."

In such ingenious fashion Fontenelle reconciles the concepts of general natural laws, the elegant simplicity of Nature's economy and uniformity, and the seeming contradiction of her incalculable diversity, to support his conjectures on the possibility of other inhabited worlds. There is, however, inherent in all this discussion of observed data, one further profound, if embryonic, concept. It appears at the very close of the first edition of his *Entretiens*. It is not merely the notion of mutability which so engrossed writers and thinkers of the first half of the seventeenth century, but an extended notion of renewal and, by implication, progress. He introduces it by using the analogy of the roses in a garden who, if they could perceive and historicize, would record no change in the gardener over thousands of generations. Fontenelle's narrator presses the point of the analogy, telling the Marquise:

The ancients took pleasure in imagining that the celestial bodies were changeless by nature, because they'd never seen them change. Had they had time to prove it by experience? The ancients were children compared to us.

He has already provided examples of change from the days of the ancients to the seventeenth century, of sunspots, of disappearing stars and meteors, of constant change in the universe. The Marquise has been convinced by his array of information, and goes further: "I expect that if the ancient stars disappear, new ones take their place. Species must replenish themselves."

The narrator finishes by averring:

I also believe that the universe could have been made in such a way that it will form new suns from time to time. Why couldn't the proper matter to make a sun, after having been dispersed in many different places, reassemble at length in one certain place, and there lay the foundation of a new world? I've all the more inclination to believe in these new creations because they correspond better to the high idea I have of the works of Nature.

It is only a step from this to the assumption that the world the Creator left to Nature was as yet unfinished, and finally that replenishment might well be improvement. Hence the unthinkable became thinkable: Creation was not complete and perfect. Here was a foundation for the concept of progress, and here Fontenelle made no attempt to accommodate prevailing theology.

As noted above, through the rest of his career Fontenelle would elaborate on these ideas that he presented somewhat rudimentarily in the *Entretiens*. However, at the time of his writing of the *Entretiens* he was still pursuing a literary career. It was more a stylistic *tour de force* than a strictly documented organization of contemporary scientific thought and when, after its warm reception in literary circles and salons, he finally moved to Paris, it was not his plan to become deeply involved in the world of science. He had, in fact, begun as a philosophical anti-Cartesian and only slowly been won over to some of the ideas of Descartes as they applied to issues concerning the nature of man. Fontenelle's developing interest in science was prolonged and only perceptible through the kind of intimate study of his life and writings made by Niderst and very recent scholars. The indications are subtle, but sufficient to demonstrate the slow shift.

The successive editions of the *Entretiens*, as one example, reveal a change of emphasis in Fontenelle's interests rather than a change of the interests themselves. By the 1687 editions he had added a sixth night of conversation which was in part a response to the reception of the work, and there were also by then a good hundred stylistic revisions to the original five nights of conversations. The editions of 1694, 1698, and 1703 show a similar attention to literary concerns, and a minimal revision of facts and figures, although some of this scientific information had been available when the first edition came out. The edition of 1708, however, has at least forty revisions which update data, and the editions of 1714, 1724, and 1742, the latter the last actually checked by Fontenelle himself, are revised on the same basis.

Another indicator is that Fontenelle's output of belles-lettres began to slow down. In 1687 he produced *Discours sur la patience* for the *prix d'éloquence* of the Académie Française. By 1697, when (after three attempts) he was appointed Secretary to the Académie des Sciences, he was producing far less in a literary vein. Then in 1699, when he began the yearly volumes of the *Histoire de l'Académie Royale des Sciences* (through to 1742) and tributes to various colleagues, his attention turned still more to scientific matters. Eventually he became an authority in his own right, obviously having absorbed rather than simply organized and summarized some of the work of his colleagues each year. He published his *Eléments de la géométrie de l'infini* in 1727 and *Théorie des tourbillons cartésiens* in 1752 (though both were apparently written some time before publication). But even though the bulk of his publications became scientific, he did not stop writing belles-lettres entirely. A volume of poems appeared in 1708 and another in 1715. Occasional verses, an address to the Académie française, a history of French theatre to Corneille, a life of Corneille, reflections on poetry, and a number of comedies are scattered through his later years. Yet clearly the weight swung from literary to scientific publication, if we add his other occasional pieces on individual scientific issues to the yearly mandatory volumes.

There is more than simple biographical validity involved in establishing this shift of emphasis in interests. The first edition of the *Entretiens* is quite distinctive in its attempt by a man of letters to bring a synthesis of scientific thought to the reading public of his day.[3] Moreover, he attempted to put it into a palatable, even enticing, form. Yet to reach and hold his audience for such a lengthy and wide-ranging dissertation, Fontenelle knew that he could not merely rely on the assumed significance of his subject.

By placing his philosopher-narrator on the estate of a young Marquise, making her unschooled in philosophy but very intelligent, quick, and witty, then limiting their dialogues to successive, moonlit evenings spent in her gardens, Fontenelle created an extremely enticing balance of instruction with flirtation, of imaginative analogue or illustration with fact or conjecture, of attack upon his society's display of man's eternal folly with optimism about the humbling effect of glimpsing infinity's real meaning.

A brief comment should be made here about a recent group whose approach to the *Entretiens,* though essentially flattering, is nevertheless misleading because of its broad criteria of assessment. It is made up of a small number of avid seekers after the "roots" of science/speculative fiction. Some have gone back as far as Lucian and Plato, moving next to medieval dream works, thence to Bacon, Kepler, all the seventeenth-century "Moon literature" writers, Swift, Voltaire, Butler, and so to the nineteenth century, where writers of short stories and novels undeniably produced fiction concerned with "science." These enthusiasts use the broadest of definitions in order to include such prestigious figures and their works, and Fontenelle is given a place among these so-called ancestors. Yet one must never confuse precedent with ancestry. Fontenelle certainly provided a precedent with his masterful presentation of scientific material in an offworld setting like the Moon, vividly illustrated by anecdotal tidbits. His work, however, is not really a speculative *fiction,* with a plot line, narrative, action and/or thematic climax and denouement. Moreover, although it may be demonstrated with fair certainty that Jules Verne was directly influenced by the *Entretiens,* and with somewhat less certainty that Wells and Poe had read it and were indirectly influenced, there is no clear evidence that the science/speculative fiction of anyone else in the nineteenth or twentieth century was influenced more than vaguely by the writings of Fontenelle or his contemporaries. What is of far greater consequence is that such a body of information and the method of using it, presented clearly and attractively to an educated public, prepared the ground splendidly for such fiction to become successful in later centuries.

Choice of the Edition

Choosing an edition of the *Entretiens* is not a simple task for several reasons. The stylist might wish to use the 1687 edition, with its cumulative literary revisions and the addition of the sixth evening of conversation, which is partly a defense of the original edition. The scientist instead might wish to use the 1708 edition containing revisions which cover an extremely active period of some thirty years in "natural philosophy." One need not, moreover, be overwhelmed by adulation to wish to present Fontenelle in the best possible light. The 1742 edition is naturally very tempting because it presumably is the last essay of Fontenelle himself at the work. It provides the final revisions and is certainly the most comprehensive and accurate from the standpoint of science. Even better might be to translate either Calame's critical or Shackleton's collated edition. Both are built upon solid rationale and acute judgment, Calame inclining slightly more to the literary and Shackleton to the scientific choice when all other factors are equal. Both supply wide-ranging introductions, displaying the broad background upon which their rationales are built, and exhaustive annotations of the texts.

Despite the various attractions of these several editions, however, I have chosen that of 1686 published in and for Paris alone, the first of the *Entretiens*. Even here there is a difficulty, since it is quite possible that not every extant edition which purports to be the very first (that is, which has the original title page) will prove to be so. Publishers of the time in both Europe and England were quite economical, and often used leftover pages for subsequent editions and printings. Be that as it may, we do have access to a sure check, since Calame cites in footnotes every variant of the authenticated first edition held by the Bibliothèque Nationale. In all doubtful cases I have deferred to this text. Admittedly, the choice of the first edition is as arbitrary as any other, but I offer the following reasons for rejecting later editions and favoring the original. By their very perfection, the editions of Calame and Shackleton become a distortion, representing a Fontenelle who never existed in life, and an *Entretiens* which is all and none of *his* editions. Any of the editions intervening between the first and the last overseen by Fontenelle may also be less than satisfactory because it is in a historical sense too transitory. That of 1742, the last word so to speak, is doubtless the most satisfactory on the basis of integrity, and yet it lacks the impact, the joy of discovery and the savor of the tour de force, which permeate the first edition. Certainly its appearance was welcome, but in 1742 its readers were influenced only in slight measure by its refinements.

It is the first edition which to me is the most significant. It is unique within its historical context, producing that ensuing wave of excitement, debate, and growing intellectual influence which occurs only at one historical moment. It was this edition which spurred, within two years of its publication, three distinct translations into English and within a short time after that, for better or worse, the emulation of lesser writers. Erroneous at times, uneven in places, it may seem in several ways less satisfactory than any of the other thirty-two editions which appeared in Fontenelle's lifetime.[4] It was written while Fontenelle was in the throes of a slow intellectual change. Nevertheless, it is historically by far the most important of the editions, and I am content to allow the reader his own assessment of the man and his work in 1686, when natural philosophy was the domain of a handful of scholars, familiar with concepts and discoveries at once fascinating and horrifying to anyone else. I have compromised, however, more to slake the thirst of the curious than to defend Fontenelle, to the extent of introducing the major revisions of the editions to 1742 in footnotes. There one may find the corrections and additions which bridge much of the gap between early and present observations and data.

A Word about Translation

Many people know of Fontenelle, are aware of the many areas of influence of the *Entretiens,* and may be impressed by or hostile to it, but have never actually read it. The reasons for this last of the seeming paradoxes are two.

First, while there are translations of the *Entretiens* into most major languages, those in English are terribly dated. There were three in the seventeenth century, one worth mentioning in the eighteenth century, and one very bad one in the nineteenth century. The only printing of an English translation in the twentieth century was that of Glanvill's *A Plurality of Worlds* (1688), a deluxe limited edition by Nonesuch Press in 1927. A facsimile of the same work was included in a partial collection of Fontenelle's works by Leonard M. Marsak in 1970. The translations of 1688 by Glanvill and Aphra Behn are by far the best, though they immediately demonstrated the differing emphases noted above. Glanvill's prose is a sinewy, competent, and quite literal rendering of Fontenelle's ideas. Aphra Behn's is more stylish, witty, and attractive. Both, however, used the idiom of the day and felt completely free to add or delete passages, substituting material which conformed to their tastes and beliefs or to those of their readers. They are a delight for the student of the period, but misleading and difficult, if not totally obscure, for the average reader today.

Second, though the fine editions of Calame and Shackleton, the latter with modernized French spelling, are relatively easy to secure, the average English-speaking reader has neither the time nor the inclination to read a seventeenth-century work in French, even assuming he has any facility with the language. A modern English translation will easily overcome both these difficulties, allow for an informed assessment of the work, and one hopes restore the *Entretiens* to its proper position of importance in both literary and scientific history.

I am painfully aware of the pitfalls of translation, especially when they are compounded by simultaneous modernization of language. When so prominent a writer and linguist as Ezra Pound attempted to translate some of the *Dialogues of the Dead* a critic responded with this admonition:

Many readers of the original have tried their hand at the translation only to discover that somehow or other Fontenelle would not "go" in English as he goes in French. The reason is not very far to seek. Fontenelle wrote a French peculiarly French, a good but untranslatable French. He must, therefore, be left and read in the original if he is to be appreciated at his intrinsic value.[5]

I make no apology for the audacity of attempting a task at which many others have not proven themselves outstanding; the *Entretiens* have for too long rested in the shadows. Their scientific and philosophic content is not insurmountably difficult to render accurately. Nor does the use of modern paragraphing make a perceptible change in content. What does disturb me is, as with those translations of the *Dialogues,* that I may fail to do justice to the inimitable style of Fontenelle. For this reason I prefer to follow the counsel of two such widely-separated translators as King Alfred and Aphra Behn, who insisted upon rendering sense for sense and not word for word. Accordingly, I have been rather free with idiomatic and colloquial expressions, knowing full well that while the style probably will not reach the witty, polished perfection of Fontenelle's prose, the intent and spirit are similar to his. I wish to bring his work to a much wider reading public. If the attempt is moderately successful, then I am certain that he would approve.

H. A. H.
Edmonton, 1989

Notes

1. Alain Niderst, *Fontenelle à la recherche de lui-même (1657–1702)*, 1972, p. 239.

2. Alexandre Calame, ed., *Fontenelle: Entretiens sur la pluralité des mondes,* 1966, p. xlv.

3. There were one or two woefully flat and pedestrian tracts which appeared even in advance of the *Entretiens,* intended for "popular reading."

4. The list below is restricted to the Paris editions, although the many published in the Netherlands may well have been supervised by Fontenelle's Huguenot relations and friends who had left France.

Paris editions of the Entretiens *overseen by Fontenelle.*

Entretiens sur la pluralité des mondes. A Paris, chez la veuve C. Blageart. 1686. Avec Privilège du Roy.

Entretiens . . . Imprimé à Paris; Et se vend à Lyon, chez T. Amaulry. 1686. Avec Privilège du Roy.

Entretiens . . . Nouvelle Édition, augmentée d'un nouvel Entretien. A Paris, chez Michel Guérout. 1687. Avec Privilège du Roy.

Entretiens . . . Nouvelle Édition, augmentée d'un nouvel Entretien. Imprimé à Paris, et se vend à Lyon, chez T. Amaulry. 1687. Avec Privilège du Roy.

Entretiens . . . Troisième Édition, augmentée d'un nouvel entretien. A Paris, chez Michel Brunet. 1694. Avec Privilège du Roy.

Entretiens . . . Par M. de Fontenelle de l'Académie Françoise. Quatrième Edition. A Paris, chez Michel Brunet. 1698. Avec Privilège du Roy.

Entretiens . . . Par M. de Fontenelle de l'Académie Françoise. Cinquième Édition. A Paris, chez Michel Brunet. 1703. Avec Privilège du Roy.

Entretiens . . . Par Monsieur de Fontenelle, de l'Académie Françoise. Sixième Édition, augmentée de beaucoup. A Paris, chez Michel Brunet. 1708. Avec Privilège du Roy.

Entretiens . . . Par Monsieur Fontenelle, de l'Académie Françoise. Septième Édition, augmentée de beaucoup. A Paris, chez Michel Brunet. 1714. Avec Privilège du Roy.

Oeuvres diverses de M. de Fontenelle, de l'Académie Françoise: contenant Les Entretiens sur la Pluralité des Mondes. Nouvelle Édition augmentée. Romme VII. A Paris, chez Michel Brunet. 1715. Avec Privilège du Roy.

Entretiens . . . Par Monsieur de Fontenelle, de l'Académie Françoise. Nouvelle Édition, augmentée de Pièces diverses. A Paris, chez Michel Brunet. 1724. Avec Privilège du Roy.

Oeuvres diverses de M. de Fontenelle, de l'Académie Françoise. Nouvelle Édition augmentée. Tome Premier. A Paris, chez Michel Brunet. 1724. Avec Privilège du Roy.

Oeuvres de Monsieur de Fontenelle, des Académies, Françoise, des Sciences, et des Belles-Lettres, et de la Société Royale de Londres. Nouvelle Édition augmentée. Tome second. A Paris, chez Michel Brunet, Père. 1742. Avec Privilège du Roi.

Oeuvres de Monsieur de Fontenelle, de l'Académies, Françoise, des Sciences, et des Belles-Lettres, et de la Société Royale de Londres. Nouvelle Édition augmentée. Tome Second. A Paris, au Palais, chez Bernard Brunet, Fils. 1742. Avec Privilège du Roi.

5. R. H. C. (A. R. Orage), *Readers and Writers* (1917–1921), 1922, p. 15.

Bibliography

Collated editions

Calame, Alexandre, ed. *Fontenelle: Entretiens sur la pluralité des mondes*; édition critique avec une introduction et des notes. (Société des Textes Française Modernes.) Paris: Librairie Marcel Didier, 1966.

Shackleton, Robert ed. *Fontenelle: Entretiens sur la pluralité des mondes *Digression sur les anciens et les modernes*. Oxford: Clarendon Press, 1955.

Ascribed Translations into English, by date

A Discourse of the Plurality of Worlds. Written in French, by the . . . Author of the Dialogues of the Dead. And translated into English by Sir W. D. Knight. Dublin: Printed by Andr. Crook and Sam. Helsham, for William Norman book-binder to His Grace the Duke of Ormond, 1687.

A Discovery of New Worlds. From the French. Made English by Mrs. A. Behn. To which is prefixed a PREFACE by way of Essay on translated Prose: wherein the Arguments of Father *Tacquet*, and others, against the System of *Copernicus* (as to the Motion of the Earth) are likewise considered, and answered: Wholly new. London: Printed for *William Ganning*, at his shop in the *Temple-Cloysters*, 1688.

A Plurality of Worlds. Written in *French* by the Author of the *Dialogues of the Dead*. Translated into *English* by Mr. Glanvill. London: Printed for *R. Bentley* and *S. Magnes*, in *Russel-Street*, in *Covent-Garden*, 1688.

Conversations on the Plurality of Worlds. By Monsieur Fontenelle. Translated from the last Paris ed. Wherein are many improvements throughout; and some new observations on several late discoveries which have been made in the heavens. By William Gardiner, esq. London: Printed for A. Bettesworth [etc.], 1715.

Conversations on the Plurality of Worlds. By Bernard de Fontenelle . . . with notes, and a critical account of the author's writings, by Jerome de la Lande . . . Tr. from a late Paris ed. by Miss Elizabeth Gunning. London: Printed by J. Cundee; sold by T. Hurst. 1803. [Apparently identical to the first printing in 1801.]

Some Major Works Concerning Fontenelle

Carré, J.-R., *La philosophie de Fontenelle, ou, Le sourire de la raison*. Genève: Slatkine Reprints, 1970.

Flourins, P. *Fontenelle, ou, de la philosophie moderne relativement aux sciences physiques*. Genève, 1971.

Labord-Milaà. *Fontenelle*. Paris: Librairie Hachette et Cie, 1905.

Maigron, Louis. *Fontenelle: l'homme, l'oeuvre, l'influence*. Paris: Plon-Nourrit et Cie, 1906.

Marsak, Leonard M. *The Achievement of Bernard le Bovier de Fontenelle*. Assembled with Translations and an Introduction. (*The Sources of Science*, No. 76.) New York and London: Johnson Reprint Corporation, 1970.

Mortureux, Marie-Françoise. *La formation et le fonctionnement d'un discours de la vulgarisation scientifique au xviiième siècle à travers l'oeuvre de Fontenelle*. Thèse presenté devant l'universite de Paris VIII—le 19 Juin 1978. Atelier national, reproduction des thèses, Université Lille III, Lille. Didier-Erudition, Paris, 1983.

Niderst, Alain. *Fontenelle à la recherche de lui-même, 1657–1702*. Paris: Editions A.-G. Nizet, 1972.

Articles or Sections of Larger Works

Bréhier, Emile. *The Seventeenth Century*. Trans. Wade Baskin. (*The History of Philosophy*) Chicago: University of Chicago Press, 1966. Pp. 292–306.

Butterfield, Herbert. *The Origins of Modern Science, 1300–1800*. [New Edition.] London: G. Bell, 1957. Pp. 122–34.

Duclaux, Mary. *The French Procession: A Pageant of Great Writers*. London: T. Fisher Unwin, 1919. Pp. 49–55.

Havens, George Remington. *The Age of Ideas; from reaction to revolution in eighteenth-century France*. New York: Collier Books, 1962. Pp. 59–77.

Nicolson, Sir Herbert George. *The Age of Reason, the eighteenth century*. Garden City, N.Y.: Doubleday, 1961. Pp. 34–52.

R. H. C. (A. R. Orage). *Readers and Writers (1917–1921)*. London: George Allen and Unwin Ltd., 1922. P. 15.

Rendall, Steven F. "Fontenelle and His Public," *MLN* 86 (1971). Pt. 2, 496–508.

Salomon, Albert. "In Praise of the Enlightenment: In Commemoration of Fontenelle, 1657–1757," *Social Research* 24 (1957), 202–226.

Conversations on the
Plurality of Worlds
Bernard le Bovier de Fontenelle

Preface

I'm in somewhat the same situation in which Cicero found himself when he undertook to put philosophical matters into his own tongue, which until then had only been treated in Greek. He informs us that some said his labors would be fruitless, because those who loved Philosophy, having already taken the trouble to seek it out in Greek books, wouldn't bother to look for it in Latin books that weren't original, while those who had no taste for Philosophy would relish it neither in Latin nor in Greek.

To this he replied that the very opposite would happen: that those who weren't philosophers would be drawn to it by the ease of reading Latin books, and that those who were already philosophers through the instruction of Greek books would be eager to see how these things had been handled in Latin.

Cicero was right to speak in this way. His superb genius and the great reputation he had already acquired guaranteed the success of this new sort of work which he gave to the public. But though my enterprise is nearly the same as his I have far less reason for confidence. I've tried to treat Philosophy in a very unphilosophical manner; I've attempted to bring it to the point where it's neither too dry for men and women of the world nor too playful for scholars. If I am told, like Cicero, that such a work is fit neither for scholars, who can learn nothing from it, nor for men and women of the world, who will have no desire to learn anything from it, I'd be far from answering as he did. It may well be that in seeking a middle ground where Philosophy suits everybody, I've found one suitable for nobody; the happy medium is hard to sustain, and I don't think I could bring myself to take the same pains a second time.

If it turns out that this book is read, I warn those who have some knowledge of Physics[1] that I don't pretend at all to instruct them but only to divert them, by presenting to them, in a little more agreeable and engaging manner, that which they already know solidly. I inform those to whom these matters are new that I believe I can instruct and divert them all at the same time. The first group will thwart my intention if they seek profit here, and the second if they seek only pleasure.

I do not delude myself[2] when I say that I've chosen from all of Philosophy the subject most apt to pique curiosity. It seems to me that nothing could be of greater interest to us than to know how this world we inhabit is made, if there are other worlds which are similar to it, and like it are inhabited too; but after all, let those who wish trouble themselves about all that; I'm certain no one would trouble himself just to please me by reading my book. Those who have thoughts to waste can waste them on such things; not everyone can afford such unprofitable expense.

I've placed a woman in these Conversations who is being instructed, one who has never heard a syllable about such things. I thought this fiction would serve to make the work more enticing, and to encourage women through the example of a woman who, having nothing of an extraordinary character, without ever exceeding the limitations of a person who has no knowledge of science, never fails to understand what's said to her, and arranges in her mind, without confusion, vortices, and worlds. Why would any woman accept inferiority to this imaginary Marquise, who only conceives of those things of which she can't help but conceive?

To be honest, this Marquise applies herself a bit, but what does applying oneself mean in this context? It's not necessary to penetrate by means of concentrated thought something either obscure in itself or obscurely explained; it's merely required that one read and at the same time form a clear idea of what one is reading. I only ask of the ladies, for this whole system of Philosophy, the same amount of concentration that must be given to *The Princess of Cleves* in order to follow the plot closely and understand all its beauty. It's true that the ideas of this book are less familiar to most women than those of *The Princess of Cleves,* but they're no more obscure; one cannot read them more than twice at the very most without grasping them very accurately.

Since I had no intention of creating a make-believe system, without any foundation, I've employed verifiable physical tenets, as many as were necessary. But fortunately it happens that on this subject the ideas of physics are pleasing in themselves and, at the same time that they're satisfying the mind, they provide a spectacle for the imagination which pleases it as much as if they had been made expressly for that purpose.

When I found some tidbits that were not entirely in this vein, I gave them exotic trappings. Virgil does the same in his *Georgics,* where he rescues the essence of his subject, which is very dry, by means of frequent, often delightful, digressions. Ovid himself did as much in *The Art of Love,* though the essence of his subject was infinitely more pleasant than anything he could mix with it. Apparently he thought it would be boring to speak of the same thing all the time, even if it were of love-making. For myself, even though I had more need than he of digressive devices, I have nevertheless used them with restraint. I've permitted them through the natural freedom of conversation, and I've only placed them where I thought readers would be happy to find them. Most of them are at the beginning of the work, because the mind will not yet have become accustomed to the ideas I'm offering. Finally, I've taken them from the subject itself, or at least from close to it.

I did not wish to make up anything about inhabitants of worlds which would be totally fantastic. I've tried to say everything one might reasonably think about them, and even the imaginings I've added to this have some foundation in reality. The true and the false are mixed here, but they are always easy to distinguish. I make no attempt to justify so bizarre a mixture; it is the single most important point of the work, and it is precisely the one for which I cannot supply a reason. The public will apprise me of what I really believe of the design I had.

It only remains in this preface for me to speak to one group of people, who will perhaps be the most difficult to satisfy; not that I haven't given them very good arguments, but rather that they may, if they wish, refuse any good arguments. These are the scrupulous people who will think there is danger in respect to religion in placing inhabitants elsewhere than on Earth. I respect even the most excessive sensibilities people have on the matter of religion, and I would have respected religion itself to the point of wishing not to offend it in a public work, even if it were contrary to my own opinion. But what may be surprising to you is that religion simply has nothing to do with this system, in which I fill an infinity of worlds with inhabitants. It's only necessary to sort out a little error of the imagination. When I say to you that the Moon is inhabited, you picture to yourself men made like us, and then, if you're a bit of a theologian, you're instantly full of qualms. The descendants of Adam have not spread to the Moon, nor sent colonies there. Therefore the men in the Moon are not sons of Adam. Well, it would be embarrassing to Theology if there were men anywhere not descended from him. It's not necessary to say any more about it; all imaginable difficulties boil down to that, and the terms that must be employed in any longer explication are too serious and dignified to be placed in a book as unserious as this. Perhaps I could respond soundly enough if I undertook it, but certainly I have no need to respond. It rests entirely upon the men on the Moon, but it's you who are putting those men on the Moon. I put no men there at all: I put inhabitants there who are not like men in any way. What are they, then? I've never seen them. It's not because I've seen them that I talk of them, and don't think that's a loophole through which I can elude your objection, simply saying that there are no men on the Moon. You'll see it's impossible that any could be there, according to my idea of the infinite diversity that Nature has placed in her works. This idea governs the whole book, and cannot be contested by any philosopher. Therefore, I believe that I'll only hear people object who talk of these Conversations without having read them. But is this any reason for me to be reassured? No, on the contrary, it's a very legitimate reason for fearing that the objection will be raised in many places.

To Monsieur L * * *[1]

You want me, Sir, to give you an exact account of the manner in which I passed my time in the country, at the home of the Marquise of G * * *.[2] Do you realize that this exact account will be a book; and what is worse, a book of Philosophy? You are expecting parties, gambling, or hunting, and you will have planets, worlds,[3] vortices; it has been a question of almost nothing but those things. Happily you are a philosopher, and you will not ridicule this as much as another might. Perhaps you will even be pleased that I have drawn Madame the Marquise into the philosophical fold. We could not have made a more considerable acquisition, for I reckon beauty and youth are always things of great value. Don't you believe that if Wisdom wished to present herself successfully to men, she would do well to take a form much like that of the Marquise? Indeed, if Wisdom could make her conversation equally agreeable, I assure you that all the world would run after her. Don't expect, however, to hear marvels, when I recount to you the conversations that I've had with the lady; it would be necessary to have nearly the same turn of mind as she, to repeat what she said, in the manner in which she said it. You will see in her only that vivacity of intelligence that you already know she has. For my part, I hold her a scholar because of the extreme ease with which she could become one. What is she lacking? To have pored over books? That's nothing; many people have done that all their lives, to whom I would refuse, if I dared, the name of scholar. For the rest, Sir, you will be in my debt. I know full well that before I go into the details of the conversations I had with the Marquise, I ought to describe to you the château where she had gone to spend the autumn. People often describe châteaux in far less appropriate circumstances, but I will spare you that. It's enough for you to know that when I arrived I found she had no company, and that I was pleased to find her alone. Nothing remarkable happened during the first two days; they were spent exhausting all my news from Paris, but then came these conversations about which I wish to inform you. I'll divide them for you by evenings, because in fact we had these conversations only at night.

The First Evening

O ne evening after supper we went to walk in the garden. There was a delicious breeze, which made up for the extremely hot day we had had to bear. The Moon had risen about an hour before, and shining through the trees it made a pleasant mixture of bright white against the dark greenery that appeared black. There was no cloud to hide even the smallest star; they were all pure and shining gold and stood out clearly against their blue background. The spectacle set me to musing, and I might have gone on like that for some time if it had not been for the Marquise, but in the company of such a lovely woman I could hardly give myself up to the Moon and stars.

"Don't you find," I asked her, "that the day is less beautiful than a beautiful night?"

"Yes," she answered, "day's beauty is blond and dazzling, but the night's beauty is brunette, which is more moving."

"You're very generous," I replied, "to defer to the brunettes when you're not one yourself, but it's certainly true that the day is the most beautiful thing in nature, and that the most beautiful things in the imagination, the heroines of Romances, are nearly always blonds too."

"Beauty is nothing," said she, "if it doesn't move us. Admit it—no day has ever thrown you into such a sweet reverie as the one you were about to fall into just now, at the sight of this beautiful evening."

"No doubt," I answered. "Nevertheless, a blond such as you would make me dream more sweetly than the most beautiful dark night in the world."

"Even if that were true," she laughed, "I shouldn't be satisfied unless the day, which is the counterpart of blonds, had the same effect. Why do you suppose lovers, who are the best judges of what stirs our emotions, address all their songs and poems to the night?"

"It's the night, of course," I said, "that deserves their thanks."

"The night hears all their complaints as well," she replied. "Why is it they don't tell their secrets to the day?"

"Apparently," said I, "the day doesn't inspire sadness and passion like the night, when everything seems to be at rest. We imagine that the stars move more quietly than the sun; everything is softer in starlight; we can fix our eyes more comfortably on the heavens; our thoughts are freer because we're so foolish as to imagine ourselves the only ones abroad to dream. Besides, in daylight we see nothing but sun and blue sky, but the night gives us all the profusion of stars in a thousand different random designs, stirring as many pleasantly confused thoughts in us."

"I've always felt that," she said. "I love the stars, and I'm almost angry with the Sun for overpowering them."

"I can never forgive it," I cried, "for making me lose sight of all those worlds."

"What do you mean, worlds?" she asked, turning to me.

"Excuse me," I answered. "You've set me onto my weakness, and my imagination is getting the best of me."

"What is this weakness?" she asked, not to be deterred.

"I'm ashamed to admit it," I said, "but I have a peculiar notion that every star could well be a world. I wouldn't swear that it's true, but I think so because it pleases me to think so. The idea sticks in my mind in a most delightful way. As I see it, this pleasure is an integral part of truth itself."

"Well," said the Marquise, "if your idea is so pleasing, share it with me. I'll believe that the stars are anything you say, if I enjoy it."

"Ah, Madame," I answered, "this isn't enjoyment such as you'd find in a Molière comedy; it's enjoyment that involves our reasoning powers. It only delights the mind."

"What?" she cried. "Do you think I'm incapable of enjoying intellectual pleasures? I'll show you otherwise right now. Tell me about your stars!"

"No!" I answered. "It will never be said of me that in an arbor, at ten o'clock in the evening, I talked of philosophy to the most beautiful woman I know. Look elsewhere for the philosophers."

Although I excused myself in this manner several times, I had to give in, but at least, for the preservation of my honor, I made her promise to keep it a secret. Then when I finally had no excuses left and decided to speak, I didn't know where to begin. To someone like the Marquise, who knew nothing of Natural Philosophy, I would have to go a long way to prove that the Earth might be a planet, the other planets Earths, and all the stars solar systems.[1] I told her several times that it would be better to talk about trifles, as all reasonable people would in our place. Finally, however, to give her a general idea of philosophy, here is the proposal into which I threw myself.

"All philosophy," I told her, "is based on two things only: curiosity and poor eyesight; if you had better eyesight you could see perfectly well whether or not these stars are solar systems, and if you were less curious you wouldn't care about knowing, which amounts to the same thing. The trouble is, we want to know more than we can see. Again, if we could really see things as they are, we would really know something, but we see things other than as they are. So true philosophers spend a lifetime not believing what they do see, and theorizing on what they don't see, and it's not, to my way of thinking, a very enviable situation. On this subject I have always thought that nature is very much like an opera house. From where you are at the opera you don't see the stages exactly as they are; they're arranged to give the most pleasing effect from a distance, and the wheels and counter-weights that make everything move are hidden out of sight. You don't worry, either, about how they work. Only some engineer in the pit, perhaps, may be struck by some extraordinary effect and be determined to figure out for himself how it was done. That engineer is like the philosophers. But what makes it harder for the philosophers is that, in the machinery that Nature shows us, the wires are better hidden—so well, in fact, that they've been guessing for a long time at what causes the movements of the universe.

"Imagine all the Sages at an opera—the Pythagorases, Platos, Aristotles, and all those whose names nowadays are dinned into our ears. Suppose that they watched Phaeton lifted by the winds, but they couldn't discover the wires and didn't know how the backstage area was arranged. One of them would say: 'Phaeton has a certain hidden property that makes him lighter.' Another: 'Phaeton is composed of certain numbers that make him rise.' Another: 'Phaeton has a peculiar attraction to the top of the theater, and he is uneasy if he's not up there.' Still another: 'Phaeton wasn't made for flying, but he would rather fly than leave a vacuum in the upper part of the stage.' And there are a hundred other notions which I'm astonished haven't destroyed the reputation of the whole of Antiquity. Finally, Descartes and some other moderns would come along, and they would say: 'Phaeton rises because he's pulled by wires, and because a weight heavier than he is descends.' Nowadays we no longer believe that a body will move if it's not affected by another body and in some fashion pulled by wires; we don't believe that it will rise or fall except when it has a spring or a counter-weight. Whoever sees nature as it truly is simply sees the backstage area of the theater."

"In that case," said the Marquise, "nature has become very mechanical."

"So mechanical," I replied, "that I fear we'll soon grow ashamed of it. They want the world to be merely, on a large scale, what a watch is on a small scale, so that everything goes by regular movements based on the organization of its parts. Admit it! Didn't you have a more grandiose concept of the universe, and didn't you give it more respect than it deserved? Most men esteem it less since they've come to know it."

"Well I hold it in much higher regard," she answered, "now that I know it's like a watch; it's superb that, wonderful as it is, the whole order of nature is based upon such simple things."

"I don't know who has given you such healthy ideas," I said, "but I'm sure few people have them besides you. Most cherish a false notion of mystery wrapped in obscurity. They only admire Nature[2] because they believe she's a kind of magic, and the minute they begin to understand her they lose all respect for her. But Madame," I continued, "you are so much more disposed to hear what I want to say that I need only draw back the curtain and show you the world.

"From the Earth, where we are, what we see at the greatest distance is the blue heaven, that great vault, where the stars are fastened like nailheads. We call them fixed, because they seem to move only with their heavenly sphere which carries them with it from the east to the west. Between the Earth and this last vault of the heavens are suspended, at differing heights, the Sun, Moon, and the five other astral bodies which are called the planets: Mercury, Venus, Mars, Jupiter, and Saturn. These planets, not being attached to the same sphere, and having unequal movements, assume diverse positions and relationships among themselves, whereas the fixed stars are always in the same relationship to one another. The Chariot[3] that you see, for example, which is formed of the seven stars, has always been made as it is now, and it will be that way for a long time. But the Moon is sometimes close to the Sun and sometimes far away, and it's the same with the other planets. That's the way things appeared to those Chaldean Shepherds long ago, whose great leisure produced the first observations that were the foundation of astronomy; for astronomy was born in Chaldea, just as geometry was born in Egypt where the flooding of the Nile, which obliterated the boundaries of all the fields, was the reason that everyone wished to invent exact measures in order to distinguish his field from that of his neighbor. As astronomy is the daughter of idleness, geometry is the daughter of property,[4] and if it were a question of poetry we would likely find that she is the daughter of love."

"I'm very happy," said the Marquise, "to have learned the genealogy of the sciences, and I can see that I must stick to astronomy. From what you've told me, geometry demands a soul more mercenary than mine, and poetry demands one much more tender, but I have all the leisure that astronomy can demand. Happily, too, we're in the country, and here we lead a fairly pastoral life, quite conducive to astronomy."

"Don't deceive yourself, Marquise," I replied, "it's not a true pastoral life merely because one talks of the planets and the fixed stars. Think how the people in *Astrea* pass their time."[5]

"Oh," she responded, "that sort of shepherd's life is too dangerous. I prefer those Chaldeans you were telling me about. Please go back to the Chaldeans. When someone had recognized this pattern of the heavens, what next?"

"It was a question," I answered, "of figuring out how all the parts of the universe were arranged, which is what the learned call making a system. But before I explain that first system, you must note, if you please, that we are all naturally like a certain Athenian madman you've heard of, who deluded himself that all the ships entering the harbor at Piraeus belonged to him. Our folly is to believe that all of nature, without exception, is destined for our use, and when one inquires of the philosophers what is the use of the prodigious number of fixed stars, when a fraction would accomplish the same thing, they answer coldly that they serve to please our sight. On this principle one could easily imagine, first of all, that the Earth had to be resting at the center of the universe, while all the heavenly bodies, which were made for her, took the trouble to turn around her and light her. Then, above the Earth was placed the Moon, over the Moon Mercury, then Venus, the Sun, Mars, Jupiter, Saturn. Over all these was the heavenly sphere of fixed stars. The Earth was placed exactly in the middle of these circles which the planets described, and these circles were greater the farther they were from the Earth; consequently the farthest planets took more time to make their round, which actually is true."

"But I don't know," interrupted the Marquise, "why you don't approve of this order in the universe; it seems clear and intelligible enough to me, and I must say it satisfies me."

"I'm proud," I replied, "that I so softened this system for you. If I gave it to you as it was conceived by Ptolemy, its author, or by those who have labored after him, it would throw you into a horrible fright. Since the motions of the planets are not so regular, sometimes going faster, sometimes slower, sometimes in one direction, sometimes another, and being often farther from the Earth, often closer, the Ancients imagined I don't know how many circles differently interlaced with one another, by which they reconciled all these bizarre observations. The confusion of all these circles was so great that, in a time when no one knew better, a certain King of Aragon,[6] a great mathematician but apparently not overly devout, said that if God had called him to His council when He made the world, he could have given Him good advice. The thought is too libertine, but it's amusing to think that the system itself provoked his sin because it was too complicated. The good advice that the King was led to give no doubt concerned the suppression of all those circles which confused the celestial movements. Apparently it also concerned the suppression of two or three superfluous spheres that had been placed beyond that of the fixed stars. To explain one kind of movement among the celestial bodies, these philosophers fashioned beyond the last sphere which we see a sphere of crystal, which imparted motion to the lesser spheres. Had they news of another motion? There was immediately another crystal sphere. After all, these spheres of crystal cost them nothing."

"And why make the spheres only of crystal?" asked the Marquise. "Wouldn't some other material have been as good?"

"No," I answered, "it was necessary that the light pass through them, as well as that the spheres be solid. It was absolutely necessary, for Aristotle had found that solidity was an aspect of their nobility, and since he had said it people took care not even to want to doubt it. But then comets were seen which, being higher than previously believed, shattered all the crystal spheres and broke up the whole universe; and it was necessary to resort to making the spheres of a fluid material. Finally it was beyond doubt, through the observations of the last centuries, that Venus and Mercury turn about the Sun, not around the Earth, and the old system is absolutely untenable by now. I'm now going to propose a different one to you which satisfies all and which will put the King of Aragon out of the running for giving advice, for it's one of a charming simplicity, which alone would make it preferable."

"It would seem," the Marquise interrupted, "that your philosophy is a kind of auction, where those who offer to do these things at the least expense triumph over the others."

"It's true," I replied, "and it's only by that means that one can catch the plan on which Nature has made her works. She's extraordinarily frugal. Anything that she can do in a way which will cost a little less, even the least bit less, be sure she'll only do it that way. This frugality, nevertheless, is quite in accord with an astonishing magnificence which shines in all she does. The magnificence is in the design, and the frugality in the execution. There's nothing better than a great design which is executed at little expense. We mortals are often prone to reverse this in our ideas. We look for economy in Nature's design and magnificence in the execution. We credit her with a little design, which she executes with ten times the necessary expense. That's ridiculous."

"I'll be happy," she said, "that the system you are going to tell me of closely imitates Nature, for this good management will aid my imagination, which will then have less trouble understanding what you tell me."

"There are no further unnecessary hindrances," I replied. "Picture a German named Copernicus, who lays violent hands on the different circles and solid spheres which were imagined by Antiquity. He destroys the first and breaks the others in pieces. Seized by a noble astronomical fury, he plucks up the Earth and sends her far from the center of the universe, where she was placed, and puts the Sun in the center, to whom the honor rightly belongs. The planets no longer turn around the Earth and enclose her in the circles they describe. If they light us, it's more or less by chance as we meet them in their paths. Everything turns around the Sun now, including the Earth, and as punishment for the long rest she was given, Copernicus charges her as much as he can with the same movements she had attributed to the planets and heavens. At last the only thing left of all this celestial train which used to accompany and surround this little Earth is the Moon that turns around her still."

"Wait a moment," said the Marquise. "You were carried away with enthusiasm and explained things in such exaggerated language that I don't think I understood. The Sun stands still at the center of the universe; what comes after him?"

"Mercury," I said. "It turns around the Sun, so that the Sun is at the center[7] of the circle it makes. Above Mercury is Venus, which turns around the Sun the same way. Next comes the Earth which, being higher than Mercury and Venus, makes a larger circle around the Sun than those planets. Finally, Mars, Jupiter, and Saturn follow, in the order in which I've named them for you, and you can see that Saturn makes the largest circle of all around the Sun, and takes more time than any other planet to make each complete turn."

"You've forgotten the Moon," said the Marquise.

"I'll find her again," said I. "The Moon turns around the Earth and never leaves her in the circle the Earth makes around the Sun. If she moves around the Sun it's only because she won't leave the Earth."

"I understand," she said, "and I love the Moon for staying with us when all the other planets abandoned us. Admit that if your German could, he'd make us lose her, too, for I can tell that in all his actions he had it in for Earth."

"He did well," I answered, "to have put down the vanity of men, who had given themselves the greatest place in the universe, and I'm pleased to see Earth pushed back into the crowd of planets."

"Surely you don't believe," she cried, "that the vanity of men extends all the way to astronomy. Do you think you've humbled me by telling me the Earth moves around the Sun? I swear to you I don't have any less self-esteem."

"Good Lord, no, Madame!" I said. "I know full well that people are less jealous of their place in the universe than in a drawingroom, and the ranking of two planets will never be as important as that of two ambassadors. However, the same desire which makes a courtier want to have the most honorable place in a ceremony makes a philosopher want to place himself in the center of a world system, if he can. He's sure that everything was made for him, and unconsciously accepts that principle which flatters him, and his heart will bend a matter of pure speculation to self interest."

"Honestly," said the Marquise, "this is a calumny you've invented against mankind. We should never have accepted Copernicus's system then, because it's so humiliating."

"Well," I answered, "Copernicus himself strongly doubted the success of his opinion. For a long time he didn't want to publish it. Finally he resolved to do it, at the urging of very reputable people, but on the same day that the first proof of his book was brought to him, do you know what he did? He died. He didn't want to rebut all the contradictions he foresaw, and he skillfully withdrew from the affair."

"Listen," said the Marquise, "we must do justice to everyone. It's certainly difficult to imagine that we turn when we never change our position, and we always find ourselves in the morning where we lay down at night. I can see, I think, by your attitude—you're going to tell me that since the whole Earth moves . . ."

"Certainly," I interrupted. "It's the same thing as if you went to sleep in a boat which was going down a river; you'd find yourself on waking in the same place and in the same relationship to every part of the boat."

"Yes," replied the Marquise, "but with this difference; I'd find the river bank changed upon waking, and this would make me see clearly that my boat had changed position. But it's not the same with the Earth, for there I find all things as I had left them."

"Not so, Madame," I replied, "not so. The shore is also changed. You know that beyond the circles of the planets are the fixed stars; there is our river bank. I am on the Earth, and the Earth describes a great circle around the Sun. I look to the center of the circle and there I see the Sun. If it didn't blind me to the stars, when I looked on a line directly beyond the Sun I would necessarily see it correspond to other fixed stars; but I easily see at night the stars it corresponded to during the day, and it's exactly the same thing. If the Earth didn't change position on her circle I'd always see the Sun corresponding to the same fixed stars; but as soon as the Earth changes position I must see the Sun against other stars. There is the shore which changes every day, and as the Earth makes her circle in one year, I see the Sun successively in the course of that year against a whole circle of fixed stars. This circle is called the Zodiac. Would you like me to make an outline on the sand?"

"No," she answered, "I can do without it, and moreover it would give my garden a scholarly air which I don't want it to have. Have I not heard of a philosopher who was shipwrecked and cast on an unknown island who, on seeing certain mathematical figures drawn on the beach, cried to those who followed him, 'Courage, my companions, the isle is inhabited; here are the footprints of men'? You know full well that it wouldn't be proper for me to make such figures here, nor have them seen here."

"True, it would be better," I answered, "if none but the footprints of lovers were seen here, which is to say your name and your initials carved on the bark of trees by the hands of your worshipers."

"Forget about worshipers, I pray you," she replied, "and let's talk of the Sun. I understand very well how we might imagine that it makes that circle which we ourselves make; but this trip takes a whole year, and the one which the Sun makes every day over our heads, how does it do that?"

"Have you noticed," I asked her, "that a ball that rolls on the ground has two motions? It goes toward the target at which it's aimed, and at the same time turns a great number of times upon itself, so that the parts on top go to the bottom and those on the bottom come to the top. The Earth does the same thing. In the time that it advances on the circle it describes in one year around the Sun, it turns on itself each twenty-four hours, so that in twenty-four hours each part of the Earth loses the Sun and recovers it. Whenever we turn toward the place where the Sun is, it seems to rise; when we begin to move away, it seems to set."

"It really amuses me," she replied, "that the Earth is taking everything upon itself, while the Sun does nothing. And when the Moon and the other planets and the fixed stars appear to turn over our heads in twenty-four hours, is this also imagined?"

"Pure imagination," I answered, "which comes from the same cause. Simply that the planets make their circles around the Sun in those unequal times corresponding to their unequal distances, and the one which we see today corresponding to a certain point of the Zodiac, or the sphere of fixed stars, we see tomorrow corresponding to a different point, partly because it has progressed on its circle and partly because we've advanced on ours. We move and so do the other planets; this places us at different viewpoints from them, and makes it appear to us that there are irregularities in their courses, of which I need not speak. It's enough for you to know that what looks irregular among the planets comes only from the diverse means by which our movements make us encounter one another, and that basically they're all quite regular."

"I consent that they shall be so," said the Marquise, "but I really wish that their regularity demanded less of the Earth; it's not good management, and for so heavy and solid a mass as it has, a lot of agility is required."

"But," I asked her, "would you rather that the Sun and all the other stars, which are such huge bodies, made an immense turn of an infinite number of leagues around the Earth every day in twenty-four hours? Because they would have to if the Earth doesn't turn on itself in twenty-four hours."[8]

"Oh," she replied, "the Sun and the stars are all fire, movement costs them nothing; but the Earth scarcely seems portable."

"And would you believe," said I, "if you hadn't any experience, that a great ship loaded with a hundred and fifteen mounted cannon and three thousand men, plus a very large number of supplies, was a very portable thing? Yet it takes only a little puff of wind to make it travel on the water, because water is liquid, yielding easily and offering little resistance to the movement of the ship. And so the Earth, as massive as it is, is easily carried in the celestial matter, which is a thousand times more fluid than water, and which fills all this great space where the planets swim. And where could the Earth be moored to resist the movement of this celestial matter and not be carried away? It's as if a little ball of wood were able to resist the current of a river."

"But," she asked again, "how does the Earth, with all its weight, support itself on your celestial matter, which must be very light since it's so fluid?"

"It doesn't follow," I answered, "that what is fluid is necessarily light. What have you to say about our great ship which with all its weight is still much lighter than water, since it floats on it?"

"As long as you have your great ship," she said as if in anger, "I don't want to say anything more to you. But can you reassure me that there's nothing to fear on a spinning top such as you make the Earth?"

"Oh well," I told her, "let's have the Earth supported by four elephants, as the Indians do."

"So here's another system," she cried. "At least I like those people for having seen to their own security by making good foundations; instead of which we Copernicans are so imprudent as to want to swim off haphazardly in this celestial matter. I'll wager that if the Indians thought the Earth were in the least danger of moving they'd double their elephants."

"That's very good," said I, laughing at her thought. "Don't spare the elephants when it's a question of sleeping securely. If you need some tonight, we'll add as many as you please to our system, then we'll take them away little by little as your confidence grows."

"Seriously," she answered, "I don't think they'll be necessary from now on, and I feel I have enough courage to dare the turning."

"You'll go much farther," I replied, "and enjoy turning, and you'll develop entertaining ideas about this system. For example, I sometimes imagine that I'm suspended in the air, motionless, while the Earth turns under me for twenty-four hours, and that I see passing under my gaze all the different faces: white, black, tawny, and olive complexions. At first there are hats, then turbans; woolly heads, then shaved heads; here cities with belltowers, there cities with tall spires with crescents; here cities with towers of porcelain, there great countries with nothing but huts; here vast seas, there frightful deserts; in all, the infinite variety that exists on the surface of the Earth."

"Truly," she said, "twenty-four hours of one's time would be well spent to see all that. And so through this same place where we are now (I'm not speaking of this garden but this same space that we take up in the air), other people pass continually who take our place, and at the end of twenty-four hours we return."

"Copernicus couldn't have expressed it better," I told her. "First the

English will pass here, perhaps discussing some political plan with much less amusement than we find in philosophy; next will come a great ocean, and there may be a ship on it far less at ease than we are. After that the Iriquois will appear, who will eat alive some prisoner of war, who will pretend not to care; then the women of Jesso,[9] who spend all their time making meals for their husbands and painting their lips and eyebrows blue to please the nastiest men in the world; then the Tartars who out of great devotion will go on pilgrimages to the Great Priest, who never comes out of a dark place lit only with lamps, by whose light they adore him; then the beautiful Circassians who will grant any favor to the first comer except what they believe essentially belongs to their husbands; then little Tartars who go and steal women for the Turks and Persians; and finally ourselves, perhaps still discussing fancies."

"It's pleasant enough," said the Marquise, "to imagine what you're telling me; but if I saw all this from above I'd want to have the freedom to speed up or slow down the Earth's movement, according to the objects that pleased me less or more, and I assure you that I'd make the politicians or those who eat their enemies pass very quickly. But there are others about whom I'm curious, for example these beautiful Circassian women; they have a custom that seems very peculiar to me."[10]

"They're so beautiful," I told her, "that their husbands find a superfluity in their favors which they freely give to strangers."

"Then the women of our country are very ugly compared to them," replied the Marquise, "because our husbands give nothing away."

"For that very reason one takes advantage of them," I answered, "whereas . . ."

"Be still," she interrupted. "I want no more of this foolishness. And a serious difficulty has occurred to me. If the Earth turns, we change air every minute, and are always breathing the air of another country."

"By no means, Madam," I said. "The air which surrounds the Earth only extends to a certain height, perhaps to twenty leagues; it follows us and turns with us. You've seen the work of the silkworm, the cocoons that these little creatures artfully fashion to imprison themselves in. These are made of very compact silk, but they're covered by a very light and soft down. In the same way the Earth, which is solid enough, is covered to a height of twenty leagues more or less by a kind of down, which is the air, and the whole cocoon turns at the same time. Beyond the air is the celestial matter, incomparably more pure, more subtle, and more agitated than it is."

"You present the Earth to me in very trivial terms," said the Marquise. "Yet it's on this silkworm's cocoon that great works are done, great wars are fought, and all around us great activity reigns."

"Yes," said I, "and all the while Nature, who takes no notice of these separate little stirrings, carries us all together in a general movement, and plays with this little ball."

"It seems ridiculous to me," she replied, "to live on something that turns and to be so upset about it, but it seems much worse not to be sure that one is turning; for in the end, to be honest with you, all the pains you're taking to show why we don't sense the Earth's motion are a bit suspect to me. Is it possible that it leaves no little mark at all by which we can recognize it?"

"The most natural and ordinary movements," I answered, "are those which give the least sensation, and that's a truth even in morality. The working of self-love is so natural in us that usually we don't even sense it, and believe we're acting on other principles."

"Ah, you're moralizing," she said. "Compared to physics, that's called boring. Let's go in: enough for the first time. Tomorrow we'll come back here, you with your systems and me with my ignorance."

While returning to the château, to exhaust the matter of systems I told her that there was a third, invented by Tycho Brahe, who, absolutely insisting that the Earth be immobile, placed it in the center of the universe, and made the Sun turn around it while all the other planets turned around the Sun, because since the new discoveries there was no longer any means of making the planets turn around the Earth. But the Marquise, who has a lively and prompt discernment, judged that it was too affected to exempt the Earth from turning about the Sun when one could exempt no other large bodies; that it was not so fitting for the Sun to turn about the Earth when all the planets turned about it; that this system couldn't be appropriate for anything but to maintain the immobility of the Earth when one had a great desire to maintain it, and certainly not to persuade one. Finally we resolved to hold to the system of Copernicus, which is more uniform and enticing and free of prejudice. In fact, its simplicity is persuasive and its boldness pleasing.

The Second Evening

The following morning, as soon as anyone was allowed into the Marquise's rooms, I sent to ask how she was, and if she'd been able to sleep while turning round. She answered that she was not completely used to this motion of the Earth, and that she'd spent the night as tranquilly as Copernicus himself. A little later people came to visit her and, after the annoying country fashion, stayed until evening. Still, we felt much obliged to them, for they also had the country right of prolonging their visit until the following morning if they'd wished to, and they had the decency not to do so. Thus the Marquise and I found ourselves free again that evening. We returned to the garden and lost no time in turning the conversation again to our systems. She had grasped them so well that she disdained to review them, and instead wanted me to lead her to something new.

"Well then," I said to her, "now that the Sun, which is presently motionless, has ceased to be a planet, and the Earth which rolls around him has begun to be one, you won't be surprised to hear that the Moon is a world like the Earth, and that apparently she's inhabited."

"But I've never yet heard anyone say that the Moon was inhabited," she replied, "except as a fantasy and a delusion."

"This may be a fantasy too," I answered. "I don't take sides in these matters except as one does in civil wars, when the uncertainty of what might happen makes one maintain contacts on the opposite side, and make arrangements even with the enemy. As for me, although I see the Moon as inhabited, I still live on good terms with those who don't believe it, and I keep myself in a position where I could shift to their opinion honorably if they gained the upper hand. But while we wait for them to have some considerable advantage over us, here is what has made me take the side of an inhabited Moon.

"Let's suppose that there has never been any communication between Paris and Saint-Denis,[1] and that a townsman of Paris, who has never been out of his city, is in the towers of Notre Dame and sees Saint-Denis in the distance. Ask him if he believes Saint-Denis is inhabited; he'll deny it heartily, saying 'I can see the people of Paris quite well, but I don't see the people of Saint-Denis at all, and I've never heard tell of them.' Someone will point out to him that of course when one is in the towers of Notre Dame one doesn't see the people of Saint-Denis, but that's because of the great distance. Everything one can see of Saint-Denis strongly resembles Paris, however; Saint-Denis has steeples, houses, walls, and it might resemble Paris in that it's inhabited as well. All this will make no impression on my townsman; he will obstinately maintain forever that Saint-Denis is uninhabited because he has seen nobody there. Our Saint-Denis is the Moon, and each of us is a Parisian who has never gone outside his city."

"Ah," the Marquise interrupted, "you wrong us. We aren't all so stupid as your townsman; since he sees that Saint-Denis is made exactly like Paris, he'd be out of his mind not to believe it's inhabited; but the Moon isn't made at all like the Earth."

"Be careful, Madame," I replied, "for if what we need is that the Moon should completely resemble the Earth, you'll find yourself obliged to believe the Moon inhabited."

"I confess," she answered, "that there would be no way to get out of it, and I see you've an air of confidence that frightens me already. The two motions of the Earth, which I had never suspected, make me timid concerning all the rest. And yet, can it be possible that the Earth shines the way the Moon does? It must, if they are to resemble one another."

"Alas, Madam," I replied, "to be luminous isn't such a great thing as you think. Only in the Sun is this a remarkable quality. It shines all by itself because of its particular nature, but the planets only light up because they're lit by the Sun. He sends his light to the Moon which reflects it to us, and of necessity the Earth reflects the Sun's light to the Moon as well: it's no farther from the Earth to the Moon than from the Moon to the Earth."

"But," said the Marquise, "is the Earth as suited as the Moon to reflect the Sun's light?"

"I see you're still on the side of the Moon," I answered, "and hard put to rid yourself of all that lingering esteem. Light is composed of little balls that bounce off solid objects in another direction, whereas they pass in a straight line through those that give them entrance, such as air or glass. So what makes the Moon shed light on us is that it's a firm, solid body, which reflects these balls to us.[2] Now I know you won't disagree that the Earth has this same firmness and solidity. Appreciate then what it means to be advantageously placed. Because the Moon is far away from us we see her only as a luminous body and forget that she's a great mass like the Earth. And the reverse; because the Earth has the misfortune to be seen from too close, it seems to us to be nothing but a great mass, fit only to furnish pasture for animals, and we don't perceive that it shines, since we can't place ourselves at a distance from it."

"It happens the same way, then," said the Marquise, "as when we're dazzled by stations higher than our own, and we don't see that in essence they're very much the same."

"It's the same thing," I answered. "We want to judge everything, and we're always at a bad vantage point. We want to judge ourselves, we're too close; we want to judge others, we're too far away. If one could be between the Earth and the Moon, that would be the proper place to see them well. One should simply be a spectator of the world, not an inhabitant."

"I'll never be reconciled to the injustice we do the Earth," said the Marquise, "and the too favorable preoccupation we have with the Moon, unless you assure me that the people of the Moon know their advantages no better than we know ours, and that they take our Earth for a star, without realizing that their home is one too."

"I can guarantee you that," I replied. "We seem to them to function regularly enough like a star. It's true that they don't see us make a circle around them, but that's not important. This is the way it is; the half of the Moon which found herself turned to us at the beginning of the world has faced us ever since; she never presents to us anything but those eyes, that mouth, and the rest of the face that our imagination has built on the basis of the spots she shows us. If the opposite half presented itself to us, we would doubtless imagine some other face from the other differently-arranged spots. It's not that the Moon doesn't rotate, but that she rotates in the same time that she revolves around the Earth, that is, a month. But while she makes a part of her rotation, and could be expected to hide one cheek, for example, of this supposed face, she makes exactly the same part of her revolution around the Earth, places herself in a new perspective, and continues to show us the same cheek. Thus the Moon does rotate in respect to the Sun and stars, but not in respect to us. They all appear to her to rise and set in the space of fifteen days, but as for our Earth, she sees it always hanging in the same place in the sky. This apparent immobility is hardly fitting for a body that ought to pass for a star, but then, she's not perfect either. The Moon has a kind of imbalance that makes a little corner of her face hide itself at times, and a little corner of the opposite side show itself. Now on my honor, she won't fail to attribute this swaying to us, and to imagine that we move in the sky like a pendulum that comes and goes."

"All these planets," said the Marquise, "are like us, blaming the others for what we ourselves do. The Earth says: 'It's not I who turn, it's the Sun.' The Moon says: 'It's not I who sway, it's the Earth.' There are lots of errors everywhere."

"I wouldn't suggest that you undertake to reform anything," I answered. "It would be much better for you to succeed in convincing yourself of the complete similarity of the Earth and the Moon. Picture these two great balls hanging in the skies. You know that the Sun always lights one half of round bodies, while the other half is in shadow. There's always one half, then, whether of the Earth or the Moon, that's lit by the Sun; that is to say it has day, and the other half has night. Note as well that as a ball has less force and speed after it's been bounced against a wall that sent it another way, so the light weakens after it's been reflected by some body. This pale light that comes to us from the Moon is the very same light of the Sun, but it can only come from the Moon to us by reflection. It's lost much of the strength and vitality with which it was received directly on the Moon; and the dazzling light which we receive directly from the Sun, and which the Earth reflects to the Moon, can only be a pale light when it arrives there. Then what seems to shine and to light us during our nights is the part of the Moon that has day, and the parts of the Earth that have day while they're turned toward the parts of the Moon that have night light them, too. Everything depends on the way the Earth and the Moon see each other. The first days of the month we don't see the Moon because she's between the Sun and us, and she moves with the Sun by day. Of necessity, all that half which has day must be turned toward the Sun, and all that half which has night must be turned toward us. We can't see that half because it has no light to be seen by, but that very half of the Moon which has night, being turned toward the half of the Earth which has day, sees us without being seen, and sees us in the same way that we see the full Moon. For the people on the Moon, then, it's the full Earth, if you'll pardon the expression. Next, the Moon, advancing on her monthly circle, moves from in front of the Sun and begins to turn a little corner of her lit side to us, and behold, the crescent. At the same time, the night side of the Moon begins to see less of the day half of the Earth, and we're waning for them."

"It's not necessary to go further," the Marquise said briskly. "I'll learn the rest when I please. I need think only a moment about it and then accompany the Moon on her monthly circuit. I see in general that on the Moon they have a month the reverse of ours, and I wager that when we have the full Moon, all the lighted half of the Moon is turned toward the dark side of the Earth, and then they hardly see us at all and call it 'the new Earth.' I wouldn't want to be accused of requiring a lengthy explanation for something so easy. But eclipses—how do they work?"

"It's not hard for you to figure that out," I answered.[3] "When the Moon is new, between the Sun and us, and all her dark side is turned toward our day side, you can understand that the shadow of this dark side is projected toward us. If the Moon is exactly in front of the Sun, this shadow hides it from us, and at the same time blacks out a part of the lighted half of Earth which was seen by the shaded half of the Moon. There we have an eclipse of the Sun for us during our day, and an eclipse of the Earth for the Moon during her night. When the Moon is full, the Earth is between her and the Sun, and all the shaded side of the Earth is turned toward the lighted half of the Moon. The shadow of the Earth is projected toward the Moon; if it falls on the body of the Moon, it blacks out this lighted half that we saw, and also steals the Sun from that lighted half that had day. Then we have an eclipse of the Moon for us during our night, and an eclipse of the Sun during the day the Moon was enjoying. What prevents an eclipse every time the Moon is between the Sun and the Earth, or the Earth between the Sun and the Moon, is that often these three bodies are not ranged very exactly in a straight line, and consequently the one that should cause an eclipse throws its shadow a little to the side of the one that should be covered."

"I'm quite astonished," said the Marquise, "that there should be so little mystery to eclipses, and that everyone doesn't figure out the cause of them."

"How true," I answered. "There are many people who, considering the way they go about it, wouldn't figure it out for a long time yet. In all the East Indies, they believe that when the Sun and the Moon are eclipsed it's because a certain demon,[4] with jet black claws, spreads them over these stars which he wants to seize; and during such times you see the rivers covered with the heads of Indians who have waded into the water up to their necks, because to them that is a very devout position and a very proper one to persuade the Sun and the Moon to defend themselves against the demon. In America they were convinced that the Sun and the Moon were angry when they were eclipsed, and God knows what they wouldn't do to be reconciled to them. But the Greeks, who were so sophisticated, didn't they believe for a long time that the Moon was enchanted, and that magicians had made her come down from the sky to throw a peculiar poisonous scum over the plants? But we, weren't we terrified not much more than thirty years ago[5] by a particular eclipse of the Sun which came? Didn't an infinite number hide themselves in caves? And the philosophers[6] who wrote to reassure us, didn't they write in vain?"

"Really," she replied, "all this is too shameful for the human race; there should be a universal decree to prohibit mankind from ever talking of eclipses, for fear of perpetuating the memory of the follies that have been committed or spoken on that subject."

"It would be necessary then," I answered, "that the same decree abolish the memory of everything and prohibit people from saying anything at all, for I know of nothing in the world that isn't a monument to some folly of man."

"Tell me something, please," said the Marquise. "Have they the same fear of eclipses on the Moon as we have of them here? It would seem absolutely farcical if the Indians of that country there went into the water like ours, if their Americans believed our Earth was enraged at them, their Greeks imagined that we were enchanted and were going to ruin their plants, and we in effect gave them back the same consternation that they cause here below."

"I have no doubt whatsoever," I answered. "I'd like to know why you think the gentlemen on the Moon should have greater courage than we have. What right have they to frighten us more than we frighten them? I believe too," I added laughingly, "that just as there have been and still are a prodigious number of men foolish enough to worship the Moon, there are people on the Moon who worship the Earth, and that we're down on our knees before one another."

"If that's so," she said, "we can certainly claim to send our influences to the Moon, and cause crises in her sick; but since it requires very little wit and ingenuity in the men of that country to destroy all these honors with which we flatter ourselves, I confess I'm still afraid that we're at some disadvantage."

"Have no fear," I replied, "there's no indication that we're the only foolish species in the universe. Ignorance is quite naturally a widespread thing, and while I'm only able to guess at that of the people on the Moon, I've no more doubt of it than of the most authentic news which comes to us from there."

"And what is this authentic news?" she interrupted.

"That which is brought," I answered, "by our learned men who travel there every day with their telescopes. They'll tell you they've discovered lands, seas, lakes, soaring mountains, and deep abysses."

"You surprise me," she replied. "I understand that one can discover mountains and abysses on the Moon, because they can be recognized by the remarkable unevenness, but how does one distinguish lands and seas?"

"One can distinguish them," I said, "because the waters, which let part of the light pass through them and reflect less, seem from a distance to be dark patches, and the lands, which by their solidarity reflect everything, are brighter places. All these different parts are so thoroughly recognized that we've given them names and these are nearly all names of learned men. There are a Caspian Sea, the Porphyrian Mountains, the Black Lake;[7] in short, the description of the Moon is so exact that a learned man who found himself there nowadays could no more go astray than I could in Paris."

"But I'd be more at ease," she replied, "if I knew in still more detail what the interior of the country is like."

"It's not possible," I answered, "for even the members of the Observatory[8] to instruct you. You must ask Astolfo, who was taken to the Moon by Saint John. I'm speaking now of one of Ariosto's most pleasant fantasies,[9] and I'm sure you'd be delighted to know it. I confess he'd have done better not to mix in Saint John, whose name is so deserving of respect, but after all with poetic license one can get away with being a bit too lighthearted. The whole poem is dedicated to a Cardinal, and a great Pope has honored it with a resounding recommendation which is prefixed to several editions. Here's the plot. Orlando, nephew of Charlemagne, had gone mad because the beautiful Angelica had preferred Medore to him. One day Astolfo, the brave knight, found himself in the Earthly Paradise, which was on the summit of a very high mountain, where his flying horse had carried him. There he met Saint John, who told him that to cure Orlando's madness it was necessary for them to make a voyage to the Moon. Astolfo, who wanted nothing more than to see that world, needed no urging, and immediately a chariot of fire appeared and carried them, Apostle and knight, through the air. Since Astolfo was no great philosopher, he was really surprised to see the Moon was far, far bigger than it had appeared to him above the Earth. It was an even greater surprise to see other rivers, other lakes, other mountains, other cities, other forests and—what would have surprised me too—nymphs who hunted in these forests. But the most unusual thing he saw on the Moon was a valley where all the things lost on Earth were found, of whatever kind: crowns, riches, renown, an infinity of hopes, the time one gives to leisure, the alms one plans to give after death, the verses one presents to princes, and the sighs of lovers."

"As for the sighs of lovers," the Marquise interrupted, "I don't know if they were lost in Ariosto's time, but today I know of none that would go to the Moon."

"If there were no one but you, Madame," I replied playfully, "you've caused all those that were addressed to you to go there, and that's enough to make a considerable number on the Moon. Well, the Moon is so precise in collecting what's lost here below that everything is there, and (though Ariosto only whispers this in your ear) everything is there right up to the Donation of Constantine. That is to say, the Popes have claimed to be masters of Rome and Italy by virtue of a deed of gift the Emperor Constantine made to them, and the truth is that no one has ever been able to say what became of it.[10] But can you guess what sort of thing one never finds on the Moon? Folly! Every bit that's ever been on the Earth is still right here. To make up for that, there are an unbelievable number of lost wits on the Moon. They're in vials filled with a most subtle liquor which evaporates quickly if it isn't sealed up, and on each of these vials is written the name of the one to whom the wits belong. I believe Ariosto puts them all in a pile, but I prefer to imagine that they're in very orderly rows down long galleries. Astolfo was quite astonished to see that the vials of many people he thought extremely wise were very full; and for my part I expect that mine has filled up considerably since I've been talking to you of visions, now philosophical, now poetical. But what consoles me is that from all I'm telling you, it's impossible that you won't soon have a little vial of your own on the Moon. The good knight lost no time in finding his own amid all the others. He seized it, with Saint John's permission, and snuffed all his wits back up his nose, like so much Queen of Hungary water.[11] But Ariosto says he didn't get far with them; he allowed them to return to the Moon through some foolish action a bit later on. He didn't forget Orlando's vial, which was the object of this trip. He had enough trouble carrying it, too, for the wits of the hero were rather heavy, and not a single drop of them was missing from the vial. To conclude, Ariosto, according to his laudable custom of saying anything he pleased, praised his mistress, addressing her in beautiful verse: 'Who will go to the heavens, my lovely one, to retrieve the wits your charms have made me lose? I wouldn't weep over my loss as long as it went no farther, but if the matter continues as it began, I can only expect to become as I described Orlando. I don't believe that to recover my wits I need to fly through the air all the way to the Moon; my wits don't range that high. They go wandering to your eyes, to your mouth, and if you are willing to have me reclaim them, let me gather them with my lips.' Isn't that pretty? Reasoning like Ariosto, I'd advise that we never lose our wits except over love; for you see they don't go far, and we only need lips that know how to recover them. But when they're lost by other means, as we're losing them right now by philosophizing, for example, they go to the Moon, and we can't retrieve them when we wish."

"As compensation," the Marquise responded, "our vials will be honorably placed in the section marked Philosophical Vials, instead of our wits wandering here, perhaps, to someone who wouldn't be worthy of them. But to complete the removal of mine, tell me, and tell me seriously, if you think there are men on the Moon, since up to now you haven't spoken of it in a positive enough manner."

"Me?" I replied. "I don't believe at all that there are men on the Moon. Look how much the face of nature changes between here and China: other features, other shapes, other customs, and nearly other principles of reasoning. Between here and the Moon the change must be even more considerable. When one travels to certain newly discovered lands the inhabitants one finds are scarcely men; they're animals in human form, still sometimes rather imperfect, with hardly a trace of human reason. He who would press on to the Moon assuredly would not find men there."

"What sort of persons would they be, then?" asked the Marquise with an impatient air.

"Honestly, Madam," I answered, "I've no idea. If it could be that we were rational, yet weren't men, and if besides we happened to live on the Moon, could we possibly imagine that down here in this place there were bizarre creatures who called themselves the human race? Would we be able to fantasize something that has such mad passions and such wise reflections; a life so short and views so long; so much knowledge devoted to insignificant things and so much ignorance of things more important; so much love of liberty and such an inclination to slavery; such a strong desire for happiness and such a great inability to achieve it? The people of the Moon would have to be extremely clever to imagine all this. We look at ourselves incessantly, and we're still guessing at how we're made. We've been reduced to saying that the gods were full of nectar when they made man, and when they came to examine their handiwork cold sober, they couldn't refrain from laughing."

"Well then, we're safely out of the way of the people on the Moon," said the Marquise, "they'll never find out about us, but I wish we could find out about them, for it's really disturbing to know that they're up there on that Moon we see, and not be able to figure out what they're like."

"And why," I asked, "aren't you disturbed about the inhabitants of that great land of Australia, which is still completely unknown to us? We're passengers, all of us, on the same ship; they occupy the bow and we the stern. You see that the bow and stern have no communication, and that at one end of the ship they have no idea of what people are at the other, nor what they're like; and you'd still like to know what's happening on the Moon, on that other vessel which sails in the skies far from us?"

"Oh," she replied, "I count the inhabitants of Australia as known, because they surely must resemble us closely, and we'll ultimately know them when we want to take the trouble to go and see them. They'll always live there and won't run away from us; but we'll never know the people on the Moon, and that's heartbreaking."

"If I answered you seriously," I said, "that one can't know what will happen, you'd laugh at me, and I'd deserve it, doubtless. Even so I could defend myself well enough, if I wished. I've a quite ridiculous thought, which has an air of reasonableness that captivates me; I don't know where it could have come from, audacious as it is. I'll bet that I am going to make you admit, against all reason, that some day there might be communication between the Earth and the Moon. Take your mind back to the state America was in before it was discovered by Christopher Columbus. Its inhabitants lived in extreme ignorance. Far from understanding the sciences, they knew nothing of the simplest, most necessary arts. They went naked, and had no weapons but the bow; they had never conceived that men could be carried by animals; they regarded the sea as a vast place, forbidden to men, which joined the sky, beyond which there was nothing. It's true that after having taken years to hollow out the trunk of a tree with sharp rocks they went to sea in this trunk, and went from one shore to another carried by wind and waves. But since this sort of vessel was frequently overturned, they were constantly having to swim after it, and properly speaking they were always swimming, except when they were exhausted. If they'd been told that there was another sort of navigation incomparably more perfect, by which one could cross this infinite expanse of water from whatever side and in whatever direction one wished, that one could stay quite still in the middle of turbulent currents, that one could control the speed at which he travelled, and finally that this sea, vast as it is, was no obstacle to the communication of people, providing only that people were there on the other side, you can be sure they'd never have believed it. But one fine day the strangest and least expected sight in the world appears. Great enormous bodies which seem to have white wings and fly on the water, which spew out fire on all sides, and which throw up on the shore unknown people all covered with iron scales, guiding as they come monsters which run beneath them, and carrying lightning bolts in their hands with which they strike to the earth all who resist. Where did they come from? Who brought them over the seas? Who put fire in their keeping? Are they gods?[12] Are these the children of the Sun? For surely they're not men. I don't know, Madam, if you grasp the surprise of these Americans as I do, but never in the world could there have been another to equal it. After that, I would no longer want to swear that there couldn't be communication between the Earth and the Moon some day. Could the Americans have believed anyone who said there could be any between America and a Europe that they didn't even know about? True, it will be necessary to cross the great expanse of air and sky between the Earth and the Moon. But did the great seas seem to the Americans any more likely to be crossed?"

"Really," said the Marquise, staring at me. "You are mad."

"Who's arguing?" I answered.

"But I want to prove it to you," she replied. "I'm not satisfied with your admission. The Americans were so ignorant that they hadn't the slightest suspicion that anyone could make roads across such vast seas. But we, who have more knowledge, would have considered the idea of traveling in the air if it could actually be done."

"We're doing more than just guessing that it's possible," I replied. "We're beginning to fly a bit now; a number of different people have found the secret of strapping on wings that hold them up in the air, and making them move, and crossing over rivers or flying from one belfry to another. Certainly it's not been the flight of an eagle, and several times it's cost these fledglings an arm or a leg; but still these represent only the first planks that were placed in the water, which were the beginning of navigation. From those planks it was a long way to the big ships that could sail around the world. Still, little by little the big ships have come. The art of flying has only just been born; it will be perfected, and some day we'll go to the Moon. Do we presume to have discovered all things, or to have taken them to the point where we can add nothing? For goodness sake, let's admit that there'll still be something left for future centuries to do."

"I'll admit nothing," she said, "but that you'll never fly in any way that won't risk your neck."

"Well," I answered her, "if you want us always to fly badly here, at least they may fly better on the Moon; its inhabitants are bound to be more suited to the job than we are. It doesn't matter, after all, whether we go there or they come here, and we'll be just like the Americans who couldn't imagine such a thing as sailing when people were sailing so well at the other end of the world."

"Have the people on the Moon already come?" she replied, nearly angry.

"The Europeans weren't in America until after six thousand years," I said, breaking into laughter; "it took that much time for them to perfect navigation to the point where they could cross the ocean. Perhaps the people on the Moon already know how to make little trips through the air; right now they're practicing. When they're more experienced and skillful we'll see them, with God knows what surprise."

"You're impossible," she said, "pushing me to the limit with reasoning as shallow as this."

"If you resist me," I replied, "I know what I'll add to strengthen it. Notice how the world grows little by little. The Ancients held that the tropical and frigid zones could not be inhabited, because of excessive heat or cold; and in the Romans' time the overall map of the world hardly extended beyond their empire, which was impressive in one sense and indicated considerable ignorance in another. Meanwhile, men continued to appear in very hot and very cold lands, and so the world grew. Following that, it was judged that the ocean covered all the Earth except what of it was then known; there were no Antipodes, for no one had ever spoken of them, and after all, wouldn't they have had their feet up and heads down? Yet after this fine conclusion the Antipodes were discovered all the same. A new revision of the map: a new half of the world. You understand me, Madame; these Antipodes that were found, contrary to all expectations, should teach us to be more cautious in our judgments. Perhaps when the world has finished growing for us, we'll begin to know the Moon. We're not there yet, because all the world isn't discovered yet, and apparently this must be done in order. When we've become really familiar with our home, we'll be permitted to know that of our neighbors, the people on the Moon."

"Truly," said the Marquise, looking closely at me, "I find you're so immersed in this subject that it is not possible that you do not honestly believe everything you've said to me."

"I'd be quite put out if you thought so," I answered. "I only want to make you see that one can support a whimsical theory well enough to perplex a clever person, but not enough to persuade her. Only the truth can persuade, and it needs to bring no array of proofs with it. Truth enters the mind so naturally that learning it for the first time seems merely like remembering it."

"Ah, you comfort me," the Marquise replied. "Your false reasoning disturbed me, but now I feel I can sleep soundly, if you'd like to retire."

The Third Evening

The Marquise wanted to engage me during the day to follow up our conversation, but I argued that we should only confide such fancies to the Moon and stars, especially since these were the main subjects of them. We didn't fail that night to go to the garden, which had become a place consecrated to our learned conversations.

"I've great news to tell you," I said to her. "The Moon I was describing yesterday, which to all appearances was inhabited, may not be so after all; I've thought of something that puts those inhabitants in danger."

"I'll put up with this no longer," she answered. "Yesterday you'd prepared me to see these people come here any day now, and today they won't even be in the universe? You'll not toy with me any longer; you've made me believe in the inhabitants of the Moon, I've overcome the trouble I had with it, and I will believe in them."

"You're going pretty quickly," I replied. "You should never give more than half your mind to beliefs of this sort, and keep the other half free so that the contrary can be admitted if it's necessary."

"I'll not be bought off with words," she responded, "let's get to facts. Are we not to think of the Moon as we did of Saint-Denis?"

"No," I answered, "because the Moon doesn't resemble the Earth as much as Saint-Denis resembles Paris. The Sun draws mists and vapors from the land and water which, rising in the air to a certain height, come together to form the clouds. These suspended clouds hover irregularly around our globe, and sometimes overshadow one country, sometimes another. Whoever could see the Earth from a distance would often notice changes on its surfaces, because a great continent covered by clouds would be a dark place, and would become brighter as it was uncovered. One would see spots changing their location, or arranging themselves differently, or disappearing all at once. And one would see these same changes on the face of the Moon if she had clouds around her, but the opposite is true. All her spots are fixed, her lighted places are always so, and there's the problem. By this reasoning, the Sun doesn't raise any vapors or mists above the Moon. So then she's a body infinitely more solid and hard than our Earth, whose most volatile elements separate easily from the rest and rise up as soon as they're stirred into motion by heat. The Moon must be some mass of rock and marble where there's no evaporation, and furthermore, evaporation is so natural and so necessary where there are waters, that there can't be any waters if none is taking place. Who then are the inhabitants of these rocks which can produce nothing, and of this land which hasn't any water?"

"What?" she cried. "Don't you remember that you assured me there were seas on the Moon which one could distinguish from here?"

"I'm sorry to say that's only a conjecture," I answered. Those dark places that are taken for seas are perhaps only great cavities. At the distance we are, it's understandable not to guess quite accurately."

"But is this enough," she asked, "to make us abandon the inhabitants of the Moon?"

"Not altogether, Madame," I answered, "we'll decide neither for nor against them."

"I confess my weakness," she replied. "I'm not capable of such perfect impartiality; I need to believe. Quickly, help me to a definite opinion on the inhabitants of the Moon. Let's preserve them or annihilate them forever and not discuss it anymore—but let's preserve them if possible. I've taken a liking to them that I'd be sorry to lose."

"Then I won't leave the Moon deserted," I replied. "Let's repopulate her to give you pleasure. Truthfully, since the appearance of the spots on the Moon doesn't change, one can't believe that she has clouds about her that shadow sometimes one part, sometimes another; but that's not to say that she doesn't exude any mists and vapors. Our clouds that you see carried through the air are only mists and vapors, which were separated into particles too small to be seen when they came from the Earth. They've met others a little colder up there, which have contracted them and made them visible by reuniting them, after which they're the great clouds which float in the air, where they remain foreign bodies until they fall back in raindrops. But these same mists and vapors are sometimes so diffuse as to be imperceptible, and only collect by forming very subtle dews that one can't see fall from any cloud. Maybe, then, vapors emanate from the Moon, for they certainly must come from her; it's unbelievable that the Moon could be a mass whose parts were all equally solid, all equally non-reactive to one another, all incapable of undergoing any change by the action of the Sun on them. We don't know any body of that sort; marble itself isn't like that; everything that's most solid alters and changes, either by the secret and invisible motion it has within itself, or by what it receives from outside. Perhaps, then, the vapors that come from the Moon may not gather around her in clouds, and may not fall back on her in showers; but only in dews. It's sufficient for this that the air (with which the Moon is apparently surrounded in her own way as the Earth is in its way) be a little different from our air, and the vapors of the Moon a little different from our vapors, which is something quite reasonable. On this basis, what with matter being arranged differently on the Moon than on the Earth, the effects would necessarily be different. But it doesn't matter anyway; from the moment we find any interior motion of the Moon's parts, or any produced by external causes, her inhabitants are reborn, and we have the foundation necessary for their subsistence. This will furnish us with fruit, grain, water, and everything we need. I mean, of course, water in the manner of the Moon, which I admittedly know nothing about, the whole proportioned to the needs of her inhabitants whom I don't know either."

"In other words," the Marquise said to me, "you know all's well, without knowing how; that's a great deal of ignorance based on a very little science, but I must console myself with it. I'm very happy again that you've given the Moon back her inhabitants. I'm very happy, too, that you've given her air of her own sort to envelop her, because it would seem to me from now on that without it a planet would be too naked."

"These two different airs," I replied, "help to hinder communication between the two planets. If it were only a matter of flying, how do we know, as I told you yesterday, that we won't fly well enough some day? I confess, though, that it hardly seems likely. The great distance from the Moon to the Earth would still be a difficulty to overcome, and a considerable one, but even if it were not there, and even if the two planets were very close together, it would be impossible to pass from the Moon's air to the Earth's air. Water is the fishes' air; they never pass into the birds' air, nor the birds into the fishes' air. It's not the distance that impedes them, it's that each is imprisoned by the air it breathes. We find that ours is a thicker and a heavier mixture of vapors than that of the Moon. On this account, an inhabitant of the Moon who arrived in the confines of our world would drown as soon as he entered our air, and we'd see him fall dead on the ground."

"Oh, how I could wish," cried the Marquise, "for some great shipwreck that scattered a good number of those people here, so that we could examine their astonishing features at our ease."[1]

"But," I replied, "what if they were skillful enough to navigate on the outer surface of our air, and from there, through their curiosity to see us, they angled for us like fish? Would that please you?"

"Why not?" she answered, laughing. "As for me, I'd put myself into their nets of my own volition just to have the pleasure of seeing those who caught me."

"Consider," I answered, "that you'd be awfully sick on arriving at the top of our atmosphere. It's not really breathable for us to its full limits, far from it. It scarcely is on top of certain mountains, and I'm quite astonished that those who are foolish enough to believe that corporeal fairies live in the most rarified air don't also tell us the reason why these fairies only make extremely short and infrequent visits to us. It's because there are very few among them who can dive, and those who can make it down to the bottom of this dense air where we are can dive only for a very short time.[2] So there are many natural barriers that forbid us to leave our world and to enter that of the Moon. At least we can try to console ourselves by surmising what we can of that world. I believe, for example, that one must see the Sun and stars there in another color than we see them. All these objects appear to us as through a natural lens which changes them for us. This lens is our air, mixed as it is with vapors and mists, which doesn't extend very high. Some Moderns contend that in itself the air is as blue as the water of the sea, and that this color only appears in one or the other at great depth. The sky, they say, where the fixed stars are attached, has no light of its own and consequently it should appear black, but we see it through the air which is blue and it appears blue. If this is so, the rays of the Sun and stars can't pass through the air without being tinted slightly by its color, and losing an equal amount of their own. But even if the air has no color in itself, it's certain that through a heavy fog the light of a torch that one sees at a little distance seems all reddish, though that may not be its natural color; and our air is no different from a heavy fog, which changes for us the true color of the sky, Sun, and stars. Only the celestial matter has the capacity to bring us light and colors in all their purity, exactly as they are. So, since the air of the Moon is of a different nature than ours, it must either be tinted with a different color, or at least be a different sort of fog, causing a different change in the colors of the celestial bodies. You see, for the people on the Moon, this lens, through which they see everything, is changed."

"That makes me prefer our home to the Moon," said the Marquise; "I can't believe that the mixture of heavenly colors there could be as beautiful as it is here. Let's, if you wish, imagine a red sky and green stars; the effect isn't nearly as attractive as golden stars on blue."

"To hear you talk," I replied, "one would say you were choosing a dress or a piece of furniture; but believe me, Nature is quite ingenious;[3] leave her the job of inventing an assortment of colors for the Moon, and I guarantee you that it will be well done. She won't have failed to vary the great spectacle of the universe from each different perspective, and always to change it in an attractive way."

"I understand her craft," the Marquise interrupted. "She spares herself the trouble of changing the ingredients for each perspective; she only changes the lenses, and so has the credit for this great diversity without the expense. With blue air she gives us a blue sky, and perhaps she uses red air to give the Moon's inhabitants a red sky, but it's the same sky all the time. It seems to me that she's put certain lenses on our imaginations as well through which we see everything and which greatly alter objects in each man's sight. Alexander saw the Earth as a nice place suited for establishing a great empire. Celadon saw it merely as the abode of Astrea. A philosopher sees it as a great planet, traveling through the heavens, completely covered with fools. I don't believe the view changes any more between the Earth and the Moon than it does here between one man's imagination and another's."

"The change of view in our imaginations is more surprising," I said, "because these are the very same objects, which people see so differently; at least on the Moon one can see other objects, or not see some that one sees here. Perhaps in that country they know nothing of dawn or twilight before the Sun rises or after it sets. The air which surrounds us and rises over us receives rays which might not fall on the Earth itself, and because it's very thick it stops part of them and redirects them to us, although they weren't naturally destined for us; it's a light that normally we wouldn't have, and that she gives us beyond our due. But on the Moon, where the air is apparently more pure, it may well be less able to redirect those rays down which it receives before the Sun rises or after it sets. You don't, then, have this gift of light which, as it strengthens little by little, prepares you pleasantly for the Sun's arrival, or which, as it weakens shade by shade, accustoms you to its loss. You're in deep darkness, and suddenly it seems as if someone draws a curtain; your eyes are struck by the full brilliance of the Sun. Then you're in vivid, dazzling light, and suddenly there you are, fallen into the deepest darkness. Day and night aren't linked by a transition which partakes of both of them. The rainbow is another thing that's lost to the people of the Moon, for if the dawn is an effect of the thickness of the air and mist, the rainbow forms in the clouds from which the rains fall, and we owe the most beautiful things in the world to those which are the most plain. Because there are neither thick enough vapors nor rain clouds around the Moon, farewell rainbow along with the dawn, and then to what can the beauteous ladies of that country be likened? What a source of comparisons is lost."

"I wouldn't have much regret for those comparisons," the Marquise said, "and I find ample compensations on the Moon for having neither dawn nor rainbow; for by the same token we can't have either thunder or lightning, because these are also things formed in the clouds. There are beautiful days, always serene, during which one never loses sight of the Sun. There are no nights when all the stars don't shine, no storms nor tempests, nor anything that seems to be the result of the heavens' anger. Can you find anything to pity in that?"

"You make me see the Moon as an enchanted abode," I answered. "However, I don't know if it's so delightful always to have a fierce sun over your head[4] with not one cloud to moderate the heat. In fact it may be because of this that Nature has sunk those things like pits in the Moon, which are huge enough to be seen by our telescopes; for these aren't valleys existing between the mountains, these are hollows that one sees in the middle of certain level plains. How do we know that the Moon's inhabitants, distressed by the Sun's perpetual strength, don't take refuge in these great pits? Perhaps they don't live elsewhere but build their towns right there. We can see here on Earth that subterranean Rome is nearly as big as the Rome on the surface. All one need do is haul the latter away, and the rest would be like a town on the Moon. A whole nation exists in a crater, and from one crater to another there are underground roads for communication between peoples. You ridicule my vision, and I heartily agree; however, seriously now, you could be more mistaken than I am. You believe that the inhabitants of the Moon must live on the surface of their planet because we live on the surface of ours. It's totally the opposite; since we live on the surface of our planet, they very well might not live on the surface of theirs. Between here and there everything must be quite different."

"It doesn't matter," said the Marquise, "I can't resign myself to leaving the Moon's inhabitants to live in perpetual darkness."

"You'd be even more upset," I replied, "if you knew that a great ancient philosopher has made the Moon the home of those souls who have deserved on Earth to be blessed. Bliss, for them, is listening to the harmony created by the celestial bodies in their motion. But as he conjectures that when the Moon falls into the shadow of the Earth they no longer hear this harmony, then, he says, these souls cry like the lost, and the Moon hurries as fast as she can to draw them from such a sad place."

"If that's so," she answered, "then we should see blessed souls from the Moon arriving here, for it would follow that they're sent to us as well, and on these two planets we believe it provides enough happiness for these souls simply to transport them to another world."

"Seriously," I replied, "it would be no common pleasure to see many different worlds. The voyage often cheers me immensely even though it's only in imagination; what would it be if one made it in reality? It would be far better than to go from here to Japan, crawling with great difficulty from one point on the Earth to another to see mere men."

"Well then," said the Marquise, "let's make our planetary voyage as we please; what's to prevent us? Let's go and visit every different perspective and consider the universe from there. Have we nothing more to see on the Moon?"

"I believe not," I answered. "At least I've shown you everything of which I was aware.[5] Going from the Moon and steering toward the Sun one finds Venus. Regarding Venus I remind you of Saint-Denis. Venus turns on itself and around the Sun like the Moon; one discovers with the telescope that Venus, again like the Moon, is sometimes waxing, sometimes on the wane, sometimes full, according to the diverse positions it's in with respect to the Earth. The Moon, according to all appearances, is inhabited; why won't Venus be too?"

"But," the Marquise interrupted, "always by saying 'Why not?' are you going to put people on all the planets for me?"

"Don't doubt it," I replied. "This 'Why not?' has a power which allows it to populate everything. We see that all the planets are of the same nature, all opaque bodies that receive light only from the Sun and reflect it from one to the other, and have nothing but the same motions; up to that point, everything is equal. Yet we are expected to believe that these great bodies should have been fashioned not to be inhabited, that this should be their natural condition, and that there should be an exception made in favor of the Earth alone. Let anyone who wishes to believe, believe that; for me, I can't bring myself to do it."

"I find you suddenly quite confirmed in your opinion," she said. "I recollect the moment when the Moon was a desert, and you didn't much care, but now, if anyone should tell you that all the planets aren't every bit as inhabited as the Earth, I can see that you'll be angry."

"It's true," I answered, "that in that moment just now when you caught me, if you'd contradicted me on the inhabitants of the planets, not only would I have defended them to you, but I believe I'd have told you what they were like completely. There are moments for believing, and I've never believed in them so completely as at that moment. Even now that I'm a bit more coolly rational, I still find it would be very strange that the Earth was as populated as it is, and the other planets weren't at all, for you mustn't think that we see all those who inhabit the Earth; there are as many species of invisible animals as visible.[6] We see from the elephant down to the mite; there our sight ends. But beyond the mite an infinite multitude of animals begins for which the mite is an elephant, and which can't be perceived with ordinary eyesight. We've seen with lenses many liquids filled with little animals[7] that one would never have suspected lived there, and there's some indication that the taste they provide for our senses comes from the stings these little animals make on the tongue and the palate.[8] Mix certain things in some of these liquids, or expose them to the Sun, or let them putrefy, and right away you'll see new species of little animals.

"Many bodies that appear solid are nothing but a mass of these imperceptible animals, who find enough freedom of movement there as is necessary for them. A tree leaf is a little world inhabited by invisible worms, and it seems to them a vast expanse where they learn of mountains and abysses, and where there is no more communication between worms living on one side of the leaf and on the other than there is between us and the Antipodes. All the more reason, it seems to me, why a huge planet will be an inhabited world. Even in very hard kinds of rock we've found innumerable small worms, living in imperceptible gaps and feeding themselves by gnawing on the substance of the stone. Imagine how many of these little worms there may be, and how many years they've subsisted on the mass of a grain of sand. Following this example, even if the Moon were only a mass of rocks, I'd sooner have her gnawed by her inhabitants than not put any there at all. In short, everything is living, everything is animate. Take all these species of animals newly discovered, and perhaps those that we easily imagine which are yet to be discovered, along with those that we've always seen, and you'll surely find that the Earth is well populated. Nature has distributed the animals so liberally that she doesn't even mind that we can only see half of them. Can you believe that after she had pushed her fecundity here to excess, she'd been so sterile toward all other planets as not to produce anything living?"[9]

"My reason is pretty well convinced," said the Marquise, "but my imagination's overwhelmed by the infinite multitude of inhabitants on all these planets, and perplexed by the diversity one must establish among them; for I can see that Nature, since she's an enemy of repetition, will have made them all different. But how can one picture all that?"

"It's not up to the imagination to attempt to picture all that," I answered. "It is not proper for the imagination to go any farther than the eyes can. One may only perceive by a kind of universal vision the diversity which Nature must have placed among all the worlds. All faces in general are made on the same model, but those of two large societies—European, if you like, and African[10]—seem to have been made on two specific models, and one could go on to find the model for each family. What secret must Nature have possessed to vary in so many ways so simple a thing as a face? In the universe we're no more than one little family whose faces resemble one another; on another planet is another family whose faces have another cast.

"We can suppose the differences increase according to the distance one travels, and whoever saw an inhabitant of the Moon and an inhabitant of the Earth would note clearly that they were from closer-together worlds than an inhabitant of Earth and an inhabitant of Saturn. Here, for example, we use the voice; there one only talks by signs; farther away one never talks at all. Here, thinking is shaped entirely by experience; there experience adds next to nothing;[11] farther away the old know no more than the children. Here we worry more over the future than the past; farther off they worry over neither one nor the other, and they may not be the most unhappy of the lot. It's quite possible we're missing a natural sixth sense that would teach us many things we don't know. This sixth sense perhaps exists in some other world where they lack one of the five we possess. Perhaps there are really a great number of natural senses, but in the division we've made with the inhabitants of other planets only five have fallen to us, with which we're content because we don't know of the others. Our sciences have certain limits which the human understanding has never been able to pass; there's a point at which they suddenly fail us. The rest is for other worlds, where some of what we understand is unknown. This planet enjoys the soft pleasures of love, but it's continually desolated in places by the violence of war. On another planet they enjoy eternal peace; but in the midst of this peace they never know love, and they're bored. To sum up, what Nature does on a small scale in the distribution of happiness or talent among men, she must have done on a grand scale among worlds, and she'll certainly have remembered to put to use this marvelous secret of diversifying things and equalizing them with compensations at the same time. Are you satisfied, Madame?" I added,[12] dropping the serious tone. "Have I spun you enough tall tales?"

"Truly," she replied, "it seems to me I've less difficulty now in grasping the differences of all those worlds.[13] My imagination is working on the plan you've given me. I present myself as best I can with extraordinary characters and costumes for the inhabitants of the planets, and devise completely bizarre shapes for them as well. I couldn't describe them to you, but nevertheless I see something."

"Let me suggest," I answered, "that tonight you give your dreams the task of devising those shapes. We'll see tomorrow if they've served you well, and if they've taught you how the inhabitants of any planet are made."

The Fourth Evening

Her dreams weren't at all successful; they kept providing something that resembled what one sees here on Earth. I had to scold her for what certain people (those who produce nothing but bizarre and grotesque paintings) reproach us for at the sight of our pictures. "Well!" they tell us, "this is all too realistic. There's no imagination!" So we resolved to forget about the shapes of the inhabitants of the planets, and content ourselves with guessing at what we could, while continuing the voyage we had begun among the worlds. We had come to Venus!

"We're quite sure," I told the Marquise, "that Venus rotates, but we don't really know in what period of time, nor consequently how long its days last. As for years, they're only eight months long, since it circles the Sun in that time. Since it's forty times smaller than the Earth,[1] our Earth appears on Venus to be a planet forty times larger than Venus appears to us; and as the Moon is also forty times smaller than the Earth, she appears on Venus to be nearly the same size as Venus appears to us."

"You distress me," said the Marquise. "I see that the Earth isn't the Shepherd's Star and the Queen of Love for Venus, as Venus is for the Earth, because the Earth seems too big on Venus; but the Moon, which seems the same size as Venus seems to us, is exactly suited to be the Shepherd's Star and the Queen of Love. Those names could only fit a small planet that's pretty, clear, bright, and attractive. It's certainly a pleasant destiny for our Moon, to preside over[2] the love affairs of Venus's inhabitants; these people must certainly understand gallantry."

"Oh, no doubt," I answered, "the humbler classes of Venus are made up of none but Celadons and Silvanders, and their most ordinary conversations equal the most beautiful of Clelia.[3] The climate is most favorable for love matches; Venus is closer to the Sun than we are and receives a stronger, hotter light from it."[4]

"I'm beginning to see," the Marquise interrupted, "how these Venusians are made. They resemble our Moors of Grenada, a small, black people, sunburnt, full of verve and fire, always amorous, writing verses, loving music, inventing celebrations, dances, and tournaments every day."

"Allow me to tell you," I replied, "that you don't know the Venusians very well. Compared to them our Moors would be like Lapps and Greenlanders for coldness and stupidity.

"But what about the inhabitants of Mercury? They're even closer to the Sun.[5] They must be vivacious to the point of madness! I believe they have no memory, no more than most savages; that they never think deeply on anything; that they act at random and by sudden movements, and that actually Mercury is the lunatic asylum of the Universe. They see the Sun much larger than we see it because they're so much closer;[6] it sends them a light so strong that, if they were here, they'd take our finest days for feeble twilights and perhaps wouldn't be able to distinguish objects. The heat to which they're accustomed is so excessive that what we have here in the heart of Africa would be enough to freeze them.[7] Their year is only three months long. The length of their day is still unknown to us, because Mercury is so small and so close to the Sun, in whose rays it's nearly always lost, that it evades all the attentions of the astronomers, and no one has yet had enough of a look at it to observe the movement it must make on its axis. But its small size leads us to believe that it completes this turn in a short time and that consequently the day on Mercury is very short, and the inhabitants would see the Sun as a great fiery frying pan suspended slightly over their heads and moving at fantastic speed. So much the better for them, for one would imagine they yearn for the night. They're lighted during that time by Venus and the Earth, which must appear quite large to them. As for the other planets, as they're beyond the Earth in the direction of the firmament, they see them as smaller than we see them, and receive very little light from them,[8] perhaps none at all. The fixed stars are also smaller for them, and there must even be many which disappear entirely—in my opinion a loss. I'd be quite angry to see this great vault adorned with fewer stars, and only to see those which remained to me smaller and of a dimmer color."

"I'm not as touched," the Marquise said, "by this loss to the inhabitants of Mercury as by the discomfort they suffer from excessive heat. I'd have us relieve them a bit. Let's give Mercury long, abundant rains to refresh them, just as it's said they fall here in the tropics during the entire four months of the hottest season."

"That's possible," I replied, "and at the same time we can refresh Mercury by another means. There are lands in China which by their location ought to be very hot, but where instead there are such great frosts during the months of July and August that the rivers freeze. This is because these regions have a great deal of saltpeter, whose vapors are very cold, and the force of the heat makes them come out of the ground in great quantities. Mercury will be, if you wish, a little planet made all of saltpeter, and the Sun will draw out of it the remedy for the very sickness it causes. What's certain is that Nature would only make people live where they can live, and that habit, combined with ignorance of anything better, serves to make them live there agreeably. It's likely they could get along on Mercury even without saltpeter and rain.

"After Mercury, you know, we find the Sun. There is no hope of placing inhabitants there. Even 'Why not?' fails us. We can assume, because the Earth is inhabited, that other bodies of the same sort must be, too, but the Sun isn't a body of the same sort as the Earth or the other planets. He's the source of all that light which the planets can only reflect to one another after having received it. Put another way, they can exchange it among themselves but they can't produce it. The Sun alone draws this precious substance from himself; he throws it out forcefully on all sides. The light reflects off anything solid it strikes, and from one planet to another it spreads long, vast streams of light which cross and recross, and interweave in a thousand different ways, to form wonderful tissues of the richest substance in the world. That's why the Sun is placed in the center, which is the most convenient place from which to distribute the light equally and animate everything by its heat. The Sun is a unique body, then, but what sort of body? We're hard put to say. We'd always believed that he was a very pure fire, but we disabused ourselves of that at the beginning of this century, when we perceived spots on his surface. Since new planets had been discovered shortly before that—I'll tell you about them—so that the whole philosophic world could think about nothing else, and eventually the new planets became all the rage, it was immediately decided that the sunspots were also planets, that they moved around the Sun, and that they necessarily hid a part of him while turning their dark halves toward us. The learned were already paying court to all the princes of Europe with these assumed planets. Some gave them the name of one prince, some another, and there was likely to be a battle among them over who would be master of these sunspots so as to name them as he wished."

"I'm not at all pleased with that," the Marquise interrupted. "You told me the other day that we've given different parts of the Moon the names of philosophers and astronomers, and I was quite happy about it. Since the princes take the Earth for their own, it's fair that the philosophers reserve the sky for themselves and rule there, but they should never permit the entry of others."

"Allow them the authority," I answered, "at least in the case of need, to delegate a star or two to the princes, or some part of the Moon. As for the sunspots, they weren't able to use them for anything. It turned out that these weren't planets, but clouds, smoke, scum rising from the Sun. They're sometimes numerous, sometimes they're few in number, sometimes they all disappear. Sometimes several join together, sometimes they separate; sometimes they're lighter, sometimes darker. There are times when we see many of them and others, equally long, when not one appears. It seems that the Sun would be a liquid material—some say molten gold—which boils incessantly and produces impurities which by the force of its activity are thrown up to the surface; there they're consumed, and then others are produced. Imagine what strange bodies these are; a certain one is as big as the Earth.[9] Judge by that what the volume of this molten gold is, or the extent of this great sea of fire and light[10] which we call the Sun. Others say that in telescopes the Sun appears completely filled with mountains that vomit flames, and that it's like a million Mount Etnas put together, but some say also that these mountains are a pure illusion, caused by something which got into the telescopes. In what may we trust, if it's necessary to distrust these same telescopes to which we owe our acquaintance with so many new objects? Finally, whatever the Sun might be, it seems entirely unfit for habitation. It's a shame; the location would be ideal. We'd be at the center of everything, we'd see all the planets turning regularly around ourselves, instead of which we see an infinity of peculiarities in their paths because we're not in the proper place to judge well, that is to say in the center of their movement. Isn't it pitiful? There's only one place in the world where the study of the stars would be extremely easy, and precisely at that point there's no one."

"You're not thinking it through," said the Marquise. "Whoever was on the Sun would see nothing, neither planets nor fixed stars. Doesn't the Sun blot out everything? Any inhabitants there would be justified in believing themselves alone in nature."

"I admit that I was mistaken," I answered. "I was thinking only of the Sun's position and not of the effect of its light; but you who've so properly corrected me, would you like to know that you're mistaken too? The Sun's inhabitants wouldn't see him at all. Either they couldn't sustain the strength of his light, or for want of being at a distance they wouldn't receive it, and all things considered, the Sun would be a home only for the blind. Once more, it's not made to be inhabited, but would you like to continue our voyage among the worlds? We've arrived at the center, which is always the deepest place in everything that's round.[11] Now we must retrace our steps and ascend. We'll rediscover Mercury, Venus, the Earth, the Moon, all the planets we've visited. Next, it's Mars that presents itself. Mars has nothing curious that I know of; its days are not quite an hour longer than ours,[12] and its years the value of two of ours.[13] It's smaller[14] than the Earth, it sees the Sun a little less large and bright than we see it; in sum, Mars isn't worth the trouble of stopping there. But what a pretty thing Jupiter is, with its four moons or satellites! These are four little planets which turn around it as our Moon turns around us."

"But," the Marquise interrupted, "why are there planets that turn around other planets that aren't any better than they are? Seriously, it would seem more regular and uniform to me if all the planets, large and small, had nothing but the same motion around the Sun."

"Ah, Madame," I replied, "if you knew what the vortices of Descartes are, those vortices whose name is so terrible and whose essence is so pleasing, you wouldn't speak as you do."

"In case my head should start spinning," she said, laughing, "it would be good to know what vortices are. Finish driving me to madness—I can't control myself any more; I no longer know how to hold out against philosophy. Let the world talk, while we abandon ourselves to vortices."

"I've never seen you so transported," I answered. "It's a shame all this should be wasted on mere vortices. What we call a vortex is a collection of matter whose particles are detached from one another and move in the same direction; they're allowed at the same time some small individual motions, provided they always follow the general movement. Thus a vortex of wind is an infinity of tiny air particles which all rotate together and envelop what they encounter. You know that the planets are carried in the celestial matter, which is both extremely fine and prodigiously agitated. This whole mass of celestial matter, which extends from the Sun right to the fixed stars, turns round and carries the planets with it, making them turn in the same direction around the Sun, which occupies the center, but in longer or shorter periods of time according to whether they're closer or farther away. Everything turns on itself, even the Sun, because he's exactly in the center of all this celestial matter, and you'll note in passing that if the Earth were in the Sun's place it couldn't do any less than to turn on itself, either.

"This is the great vortex of which the Sun is like the master, but at the same time the planets make up little individual vortices in imitation of the Sun's. Each of them, while turning around the Sun, never stops turning on its axis, and carries with it in the same direction a certain quantity of the celestial matter, which is always ready to follow any motion one wishes to give it as long as it's not diverted from its general motion. This is the distinctive vortex of the planet, and it extends as far as the strength of the planet's motion can exert itself. If it happens that some smaller planet falls into the vortex dominated by the larger planet, it's carried away and forced irrevocably to turn around it, while the whole assembly, the large planet, the small, and the vortex which encloses them, revolves in turn about the Sun. That's how at the world's beginning we made the Moon follow us, because she found herself within the limits of our vortex and totally at our disposal. Jupiter, which I had begun to speak about to you, was more fortunate or more powerful than we were; there were four little planets in its neighborhood and it subjugated all four. We who are a major planet, do you know what we'd have been if we'd found ourselves close to Jupiter?

It's ninety times[15] bigger than we are; it would have swallowed us into its vortex with no difficulty, and we'd be merely a moon dependent upon it, instead of which we've a Moon in our own vortex. How true it is that chance alone often decides one's whole fortune."

"And what assures us," said the Marquise, "that we'll always remain where we are? I begin to fear that we might have the folly to approach a planet as enterprising as Jupiter, or that it might come toward us to absorb us, for it seems to me that in this great movement where you say the celestial matter is, the planets must be irregularly agitated, sometimes approaching, sometimes receding from one another."

"We could gain as well as lose at that game," I replied. "Perhaps we might subject Mercury and Venus[16] to our domination which are smaller planets. But we've nothing to hope or to fear, either; the planets stay where they are and new conquests are denied them, as they once were to the kings of China. You know very well that when one puts oil with water the oil floats. When one places an extremely light body on top of these two liquids, the oil supports it and won't go into the water. When one puts in another, heavier body of a precise density, it will pass through the oil, which is far too weak to stop it, and fall to where it encounters the water, which has the strength to support it. Thus in this liquid composed of two liquids which won't mix, two unequally heavy bodies will arrive naturally at two different places, and never will one rise or the other descend. When one takes other liquids which remain separated, and throws in other bodies, the same thing will happen. Imagine that the celestial matter which fills the great vortex has different layers that envelop one another, whose weights are different, like those of oil and water and other liquids. The planets also have different weights, so that each one consequently stops at the layer which has precisely the strength necessary to support it and give it equilibrium, and you can see it's impossible that it should ever leave."

"I understand," said the Marquise, "that the weights of things regulate the ranks very well. Would to God that there were something similar to regulate us, which would fix people in those positions to which they're suited by nature. See how relaxed I am now, near Jupiter. I'm satisfied that it will leave us in our little vortex with our own single Moon. I'm in a charitable mood and no longer envy it those four moons that it has."

"You'd be wrong to envy it those," I replied. "Jupiter has no more than it needs. At the distance it is from the Sun,[17] its moons receive and reflect to it only a rather feeble light. The number makes up for the slight effect of each. It's true that since Jupiter turns on itself in ten hours and the nights, which consequently last only five, are short, four moons might not seem so necessary,[18] but there's something else to consider. Here, under our poles, we have six months of day and six months of night. This is because the poles are the two extremities of Earth farthest from the places where the Sun gives direct light, and over which it seems to take its course. The Moon keeps, or seems to keep, nearly the same course as the Sun, and just as the inhabitants of the poles see the Sun during all of one half of its journey of a year, and during the other half don't see it at all, they also see the Moon during all one half of her monthly circuit, that is to say fifteen days, and don't see her at all during the other half. Jupiter's years equal twelve of ours, and there must be on this planet two opposite extremities where there are days and nights of six entire years. Six-year nights are very long, so it's principally for them, I believe, that the four moons were made. The one that's highest in regard to Jupiter makes its revolution around it in seventeen days, the second in seven, the third in three-and-a-half, the fourth in forty-two hours. Their orbits being exactly halved for those unfortunate creatures who have six years of night, only twenty-one hours can pass when one doesn't see at least the last moon appear. That's some consolation during such dreary, endless darkness, but wherever one lives on Jupiter those four moons provide the prettiest sights in the world. Sometimes all four rise together and then separate according to the inequality of their orbits; sometimes they're all at their meridian, one above the other; sometimes one sees them all on the horizon at equal distances; sometimes when two rise, two set. Most of all, I'd like to see the game of perpetual eclipses they play, for never a day goes by when they don't eclipse one another, or don't eclipse the Sun; and assuredly, since eclipses are so familiar in that world, they're a subject of amusement and not fear, as they are here."

"And you'll not fail," the Marquise asked, "to populate these four moons, even though they're merely subordinate little planets, destined only to light another planet during its nights?"

"Never doubt it," I answered. "These planets are no less worthy of being inhabited for having the misfortune of being assigned to turn about another of greater importance."

"I'd wish then," she replied, "that the inhabitants of the four moons of Jupiter were like its colonies, that they'd receive from it, if possible, their laws and their customs, and that consequently they'd give it some sort of homage, and regard the great planet with nothing but respect."

"Wouldn't it also follow," I said to her, "that the four moons should send ambassadors to Jupiter from time to time, to make it an oath of allegiance? Well, I must confess that the lack of domination we have over the people of our Moon makes me doubt that Jupiter has very much over the inhabitants of its moons, and I believe that one of the advantages to which it can most reasonably aspire is to make them afraid. For example, on the closest moon to it, Jupiter appears three hundred and sixty times[19] greater than our Moon seems to us, for it's that much larger. It is, I believe, much closer to them than ours is to us, which makes it larger still. So they always have this monstrous planet hanging over their heads, and not very far away. Truly, if the Gauls of old feared that the sky would fall on them, the inhabitants of that moon should have much more reason to fear the fall of Jupiter!"

"Maybe that's what they fear," she said, "instead of eclipses, from which fear you've assured me they're exempt. One folly must surely be replaced by another."

"It's absolutely necessary," I agreed. "The inventor of the third system of which I told you the other night, the celebrated Tycho Brahe, one of the greatest astronomers who ever lived, never feared eclipses as the common people feared them; he spent his life with them. But would you believe what he feared instead? If, when he left his lodgings, the first person he met was an old woman, or if a hare crossed his path, Tycho Brahe believed that the day would be unlucky and went promptly back home to shut himself up, without having done a single thing."

"It wouldn't be just," she replied, "after that man was unable to free himself from fear of eclipses with impunity, that the inhabitants of this moon of Jupiter we were speaking of should get off more lightly. Let's give them no quarter; they'll submit to the universal law, and fall into some other [fear]. But since I won't take the trouble to guess what it might be, please clear up another difficulty for me which has bothered me for several minutes. If the Earth is so small compared to Jupiter, does Jupiter see us? I'm afraid we may be unknown to it."

"To be honest, I believe that," I answered. "Jupiter would have to see the Earth ninety times[20] smaller than we see it. It's too small to be seen. Here's the only thing we can believe in our favor. There'll be astronomers on Jupiter who, after taking great pains to construct excellent telescopes, and choosing the finest nights to observe, will finally discover in the heavens a tiny planet that they've never seen before. First the *Philosophers' Journal* of that country will speak of it; the people of Jupiter either never understand anything about it or do nothing but laugh at it. The philosophers, whose judgments are destroyed by this, decide to believe none of it, and there are only a few very reasonable people who are willing to consider it. They observe again, they see the little planet again, they're convinced it isn't a fantasy; they even begin to suspect that it moves about the Sun. They find at the end of a thousand observations that this movement is one year long, and finally, thanks to all the pains the scholars have taken, they know on Jupiter that our Earth is a planet. The curious run to view it at the end of a telescope, which can hardly catch sight of it again."

"If it weren't," said the Marquise, "that it's not very agreeable to know that on Jupiter they can't discover us without telescopes, I could imagine with pleasure these telescopes aimed at us, as ours are toward them, and the mutual curiosity with which the planets consider one another and ask among themselves, 'What world is that? What people live on it?'"

"This doesn't happen as quickly as you think," I replied. "Even if they saw our Earth on Jupiter and knew about it there, still we're not our Earth; they wouldn't have the faintest suspicion that it could be inhabited. If anyone were to think of it, heaven knows how all Jupiter would laugh at him. It's possible we're the cause of philosophers being prosecuted there who have tried to insist that we exist. However, I'm more inclined to believe that the inhabitants of Jupiter are too occupied in making discoveries on their own planet to daydream at all about ours. It's so large that, if they can sail, their Christopher Columbus[21] won't lack employment. People of that world could hardly know a hundredth of the other peoples even by reputation, whereas on Mercury, which is quite small, they're all neighbors; they live intimately together and consider a tour of their world a mere stroll.

"If they can't see us on Jupiter, consider that they can see Venus and Mercury even less, worlds still smaller and farther from them. In compensation, its inhabitants see Mars, and their four moons and Saturn with its moons. That's enough planets to confuse those among them who are astronomers; Nature has had the kindness to hide the rest of the universe from them."

"What?" said the Marquise. "You call that a kindness?"

"Undoubtedly," I answered. "There are sixteen planets in the whole great vortex. Nature, who wishes to save us the trouble of studying all their movements, only shows us seven; isn't this a great favor? But we who don't appreciate the value of it, we work so hard that we find the other nine that were hidden from us, and then we're punished by the great efforts that astronomy demands now."

"I see," she answered, "by the number of sixteen planets, that Saturn must have five moons."[22]

"It does indeed," I replied,[23] "and of these five moons two are newly discovered. But there's something else which is still more remarkable. As its year equals thirty of ours, and consequently it has countries where a single night lasts fifteen whole years, guess what Nature has invented to light such dreadful nights. She's not content to give five moons to Saturn, she's placed a great circle or ring about it which surrounds it completely and which, being placed high enough to be free of the shadow of the body of the planet, reflects the light of the Sun perpetually into places which can't see it."

"Truly," said the Marquise (like a person coming to, with astonishment), "all this is magnificently arranged; it really seems that Nature has had the needs of some living beings in view, and that the distribution of moons wasn't made haphazardly. They were only doled out to the planets farthest from the Sun: the Earth, Jupiter, Saturn; for it wasn't worthwhile to give them to Venus and Mercury, who receive only too much light, whose nights are very short and are apparently considered greater benefits of nature than the days themselves. But wait! It seems to me that Mars, which is in fact farther from the Sun than the Earth, hasn't any moon."

"No one can pretend otherwise," I answered. "It has none, and it must have resources for its night that we don't know. You've seen phosphors, dry or liquid materials which on receiving sunlight drink it in and are filled by it, and later throw a fairly bright light into the darkness. Perhaps Mars has high rocky peaks that are natural phosphorus and take in a supply of light during the day which they give off during the night. You can't deny it would be a pretty grand spectacle to see all those rocks lighting up on all sides as soon as the Sun set, and providing quite naturally magnificent illumination. You also know that in America there are birds so luminous at night that one can use them to read by. How do we know that Mars hasn't a great number of these birds which scatter in all directions as soon as night falls and spread a new day?"

"I'm not content," she replied, "with either your rocks or your birds. These would certainly be attractive, but since Nature has given so many moons to Saturn and Jupiter, it's an indication that they're necessary. I'd have been satisfied that all the worlds farthest from the Sun had them, if Mars hadn't come along and made us a disagreeable exception."

"Really," I answered, "if you were more involved with Philosophy than you are, you'd have to become accustomed to seeing exceptions in the best of systems. There's always something that fits your system like a glove, and then something that you have to fit in as best you can, or else leave out if you ever hope to see the end of it. Let's do the same for Mars, since it's not profitable for us, and say no more about it. We'd be quite astonished if we were on Saturn to see this great ring over our heads during the night, forming a semi-circle from one end of the horizon to the other and reflecting the sunlight to give the effect of a continuous moon."

"And aren't we going to put inhabitants into this great ring?" the Marquise interrupted, laughing.

"Although I'm in the mood," I answered, "to send them everywhere rashly enough, I admit I wouldn't dare put any there; this ring seems to me too irregular a habitation. We can hardly help populating the five little moons. If, however, as some suspect, the ring is nothing but a circle of moons which follow one another very closely and have exactly the same motion, and the little moons are fugitives from that great circle, how many worlds must there be in the vortex of Saturn! Whatever the case may be, the people of Saturn are badly enough off even with the aid of the ring. It gives them light, but what sort of light at that distance from the Sun! The Sun itself is only a little star for them, white and pale, with the feeblest of brightness and heat. If we placed them in our coldest countries, in Greenland or Lapland, we'd see them sweat huge drops and die of the heat."

"You give me an idea of Saturn which freezes me," said the Marquise, "and a little while ago you were setting me on fire when you spoke of Mercury."

"It's necessary," I said, "that the two worlds which are at the two extremities of this great vortex should be opposite in all things."

"Therefore," she replied, "they're very wise on Saturn, for you told me that everyone was mad on Mercury."

"If they're not very wise on Saturn," I returned, "at least by all appearances they're quite phlegmatic. These are people who don't know what it is to laugh, who always take a day to answer the slightest question asked them, and who would have found Cato of Utica too playful and frisky."

"I've had a thought," she said. "All the inhabitants of Mercury are lively, all those of Saturn are slow. Among us some are lively, some slow; couldn't that be because our Earth, being precisely in the middle of these other worlds, shares in both extremes? There's no fixed and definite character for men; some are made like the inhabitants of Mercury, other like those of Saturn, and we're a mixture of all the species that are found in the other planets."

"I like this idea well enough," I replied. "We form such a bizarre collection that one could believe we were assembled from many different worlds. In fact it's quite convenient to be here, where we can see all the other worlds in summary."

"At least," the Marquise answered, "one very real convenience of the location of our world is that it's neither so hot as Mercury or Venus, nor so cold as Jupiter or Saturn. Moreover, we're in a place on the Earth where we feel no excess of heat or cold. Truly, if a certain philosopher could give thanks to Nature for being a man, not a beast, Greek and not barbarian,[24] I too can give thanks to her for being on the most temperate planet in the universe, and in one of the most temperate spots on this planet."

"If you listen to me, Madame," I said, "you'll give thanks to her for being young and not old, young and beautiful and not young and ugly; young and beautiful and French, and not young, beautiful, and Italian. There are many other things to be thankful for besides the ones you chose of the position of your vortex or the temperature of your country."

"Good heavens," she retorted, "let me be grateful for everything, including the vortex in which I'm placed. The measure of happiness which has been given to us is small enough; we mustn't lose any of it, and it's good to have a taste for the most common, least important things which make them worthwhile. If we wanted only intense pleasures, we'd have few of them, we'd wait a long time for them, and we'd pay dearly for them."

"Can you promise me," I replied, "that if anyone offered you these intense pleasures you'd remember the vortices and me, and not shut yourself away from us?"

"Yes," she answered, "but you must make sure that Philosophy always furnishes me with new pleasures."

"At least for tomorrow," I replied, "I can hope they'll not be lacking. I've the fixed stars, which surpass all that you've seen up to now."

The Fifth Evening

The Marquise was really impatient to know what might happen with the fixed stars. "Will they be inhabited like the planets," she asked me, "or not? What will we make of them?"

"You could probably guess if you really wanted to," I said. "The fixed stars can't be less distant from the Earth than fifty million leagues or so,[1] and if you were to anger an astronomer he'd put them still farther away. The distance from the Sun to the farthest planet is nothing in comparison with the distance from the Sun or the Earth to the fixed stars, and one doesn't take the trouble to compute it. Their light, as you see, is bright and sparkling enough. If they received it from the Sun, it would have to be a very feeble light after a trip of fifty million leagues, and they would have to send it back across this same distance by reflection, which would weaken it that much more. It would be impossible for a light that had to suffer reflection, and go twice fifty million leagues, to have the strength and brightness of the fixed stars' light. So they must be self-illuminated and all of them, in a word, so many Suns."

"Would I be tricking myself," the Marquise cried, "or do I see where you want to lead me? Are you going to tell me 'The fixed stars are suns, too; our Sun is the center of a vortex which rotates around it; why shouldn't each fixed star also be the center of a vortex which moves about it? Our Sun has planets which it lights; why shouldn't each fixed star have some which it lights, too?"

"I can only answer," I told her, "what Phaedra said to Oenone: 'You said it!'"

"But," she replied, "here's a universe so large that I'm lost, I no longer know where I am, I'm nothing. What, is everything to be divided into vortices, thrown together in confusion? Each star will be the center of a vortex, perhaps as large as ours? All this immense space which holds our Sun and our planets will be merely a small piece of the universe? As many spaces as there are fixed stars? This confounds me—troubles me—terrifies me."

"And as for me," I answered, "this puts me at my ease. When the sky was only this blue vault, with the stars nailed to it, the universe seemed small and narrow to me; I felt oppressed by it. Now that they've given infinitely greater breadth and depth to this vault by dividing it into thousands and thousands of vortices, it seems to me that I breathe more freely, that I'm in a larger air, and certainly the universe has a completely different magnificence. Nature has held back nothing to produce it; she's made a profusion of riches altogether worthy of her. Nothing is so beautiful to visualize as this prodigious number of vortices, each with a sun at its center making planets rotate around it. The inhabitants of a planet in one of these infinite vortices see on all sides the lighted centers of the vortices surrounding them, but aren't able to see their planets which, having only a feeble light borrowed from their sun, don't send it beyond their own world."

"You offer me," she said, "a kind of perspective so long that my eyes can't reach the end of it. I see the Earth's inhabitants clearly; next you make me see those of the Moon and the other planets of our vortex clearly enough, it's true, though less clearly than those of Earth. After them come the inhabitants of the planets of the other vortices who are, I must confess, completely in the dark. Whatever effort I make to see them, I can hardly perceive them at all. And in effect, aren't they nearly annihilated by the phrase you have to use in speaking of them? You're forced to call them 'inhabitants of one of the planets of one of these infinite vortices.' We ourselves, to whom the same phrase applies—admit that you'd scarcely know how to pick us out in the middle of so many worlds. As for me, I'm beginning to see the Earth so frighteningly small that I believe hereafter I'll never be impressed by another thing. Assuredly, if people have such a love of acquisition, if they make up plan after plan, if they go to so much trouble, it's because they don't know about vortices. I can claim that my new enlightenment justifies my laziness, and when anyone reproaches me for my indolence I'll answer: 'Ah, if you knew what the fixed stars are!'"

"Alexander must not have known," I replied, "for a certain author who holds that the Moon is inhabited says very seriously that it's impossible for Aristotle not to have held such a reasonable opinion (for how could a truth have escaped Aristotle?), but that he never wanted to speak of it for fear of displeasing Alexander, who would have been in despair to see a world which he was unable to conquer. All the more reason for concealing the fixed stars and their vortices from him, if anyone had known about them in those times; it would have meant failure at court to mention them to him. I, who know of them, am most annoyed that I can't derive any use from my knowledge. They can cure nothing more, according to your reasoning, than ambition and restlessness, and I've neither of these sicknesses. A little weakness for that which is beautiful, that's my sickness, and I don't believe the vortices do anything for that. The other worlds may make this one little to you, but they don't spoil lovely eyes, or a beautiful mouth; those have their full value despite all the possible worlds."

"Love is a strange thing," she laughed. "It escapes everything, and there's not one system that can do it harm. But tell me frankly, is your system really true? Don't conceal anything; I'll keep your secret. It seems to me that it's founded on a very flimsy expediency. A fixed star is self-illuminated like the Sun, and consequently like the Sun it must be the center and soul of a vortex and have planets that rotate around it. Is this absolutely necessary?"

"Listen, Madame," I answered, "since we're inclined to keep mixing foolish lovetalk with our serious conversation, the logic of mathematics is like that of love. You can't grant a lover the least favor without soon having to grant more, and still more, and in the end it's gone awfully far. Well, if you grant a mathematician the least principle, he'll draw a conclusion from it that you must grant him too, and from that conclusion another, and in spite of yourself he'll lead you so far you'll have trouble believing it. These two kinds of people always take more than one gives them. You agree that when things seem alike to me in all apparent ways, I can then believe they're equally alike in ways that aren't apparent, if there's nothing there to hinder me. From that I've concluded that the Moon's inhabited because it resembles the Earth, the other planets because they resemble the Moon. I find that the fixed stars resemble our Sun; I attribute all it has to them. You're too involved to be able to retreat; you must take the hurdle with good grace."

"But," she said, "on the basis of this resemblance that you establish between the fixed stars and our Sun, the people of another great vortex see the Sun merely as a little fixed star, which appears to them only at night."

"This is beyond doubt," I replied. "Our Sun is so close to us in comparison with the suns of other vortices that its light must have infinitely greater impact on our eyes than theirs. When we see it, we see nothing but it, and it blots out everything, but in another great vortex it's another sun that dominates, and in turn blots out ours, which only appears there during the night with the rest of the alien suns—that is to say the fixed stars. They attach it along with the others to the great vault of heaven, and there it makes up part of some bear or some bull. As for the planets which revolve around it, our Earth for example, since they never see them from so far away they never even dream of them. So all the suns are daytime suns for the vortex in which they're placed, and nighttime suns for all the other vortices. In their own systems they're unique, one of a kind, but elsewhere they only add to the multitude."

"Nevertheless," she replied, "may these systems not, despite this similarity, differ in a thousand ways? After all, a basic resemblance doesn't exclude infinite differences."

"Definitely," I answered. "But the difficulty is to figure it out. What do I know? One vortex has more planets revolving around its sun, another has fewer. In one there are subordinate planets which revolve around the larger planets; in another there are none. Here they're gathered around their sun like a little platoon, beyond which a great void extends, stretching to neighboring vortices; elsewhere they travel around the edges of the vortex and leave the middle empty. I don't doubt that there may be some vortices deserted and without planets, others whose sun, being off-center, has an orbit itself and carries its planets with it, others whose planets rise or fall with respect to their sun by the changing equilibrium which keeps them suspended. What do you want from me? That's enough for a man who's never left his own vortex."

"It's hardly enough for the quantity of worlds," she said. "What you say will suffice for only five or six, and from here I can see thousands."

"How would it be, then," I answered, "if I told you that there are many more fixed stars than you see, that with telescopes we discover an infinite number that don't appear to the naked eye, and that in a single constellation where we've counted perhaps twelve or fifteen, more are found than we've seen up to now in the whole sky?"

"Have mercy," she cried. "I give up! You overwhelm me with systems and vortices."

"And I know," I added, "what I'm still holding back from you. You see that whiteness that's called the Milky Way. Can you guess what it is? An infinity of small stars, invisible to the eyes because they're so small and strewn so close to one another that they seem to form a continuous whiteness. I wish you could view this anthill of stars, this seeding of worlds, if these expressions are permitted, with a telescope. In some ways it resembles the Maldivian Islands, those twelve thousand little islands or banks of sand, separated merely by sea channels which one may leap almost like a ditch. Thus the little vortices of the Milky Way are so close that it seems to me one could talk from one system to the other or even shake hands. At least, I believe, the birds of one system can cross easily to another, and they can train pigeons to carry letters as one does here in the Levant from one town to another. These little systems apparently are exceptions to the general rule that one sun in its own vortex blots out all alien suns as soon as it appears. If you're in one of the little vortices of the Milky Way, your sun isn't much closer to you and consequently hasn't appreciably more effect on your eyes than a hundred thousand other suns of the neighboring vortices. So you see your sky glow with an infinite number of fires that are very close to one another and not far from you. When you lose sight of your particular sun, enough remain for you, and your night is no less bright than the day; at least the difference can't be perceptible, and to speak more precisely, you never have night. They'd be quite astonished, the people of those systems, accustomed as they are to perpetual light, if they were told there were unfortunates who have true nights, who fall into very deep darkness and who, when they do enjoy the light, see only one solitary sun. They'd regard us as outcasts of nature and shudder with horror at our situation."[2]

"I won't ask you," said the Marquise, "if there are moons among the systems of the Milky Way. I see clearly that there'd be no use for them on the principal planets that have no night, and that move besides in space too confined to burden themselves with this baggage of subordinate planets. But do you know that by multiplying the systems so liberally for me, you're bringing to light a real difficulty? The vortices whose suns we see touch the vortex where we are. The vortices are round, aren't they? How can so many globes touch a single one? I want to imagine this, and I realize that I can't."

"You show your intelligence," I answered, "by having this difficulty, and even by not being able to resolve it, for it's quite sound in itself, and, in the manner you conceive it, it's unanswerable; and it shows very little intelligence to find answers to something that has none. If our vortex were in the shape of a die, it would have six flat faces and would be far from round; but against each of these faces one could place a vortex of similar shape. If in place of six flat faces there were twenty, fifty, a thousand, there'd be up to a thousand vortices which could rest against it, each on a face, and you well know that the more flat faces a body has on its outside the closer it comes to being round. A diamond cut with facets on all sides, if the facets were very small, would be almost as round as a pearl of equal size. The vortices are only round in this manner. They have an infinity of faces on the outside, each of which conjoins another vortex. These faces are quite unequal; here they're larger, there smaller. The smallest on our vortex, for example, correspond to the Milky Way, and hold all those little systems. When two vortices that connect by their adjacent faces leave some slight void beneath where they meet, as must often happen, then Nature, who manages her territory well, will fill the void for you with a little vortex or two, perhaps with a thousand, that don't inconvenience the others and still remain one, two, or a thousand systems more. Thus we can see many more systems than our vortex has faces to touch. I bet that although these little systems were only made to be thrown into the corners of the universe which would otherwise have been useless, and although they're unknown to the other systems that touch them, they're nonetheless quite content with themselves. These are doubtless the ones whose little suns one can only discover with a telescope, and which are so plentiful. Finally, all these vortices adjust to one another in the best possible way, and as each must turn around its own sun without changing its place, each takes the method of turning which is the most comfortable and easy in its situation. They engage one another somewhat like the gears of a watch, and help one another in their motions. Still, it's true that they also work against one another. Each world, so they say, is like a balloon which would inflate and expand itself if one would let it, but it's immediately rebuffed by the neighboring systems and it subsides, after which it begins to inflate again, and so on; and some maintain that the fixed stars display a trembling light, and seem bright and dim, simply because their vortices perpetually press against ours and are perpetually repelled."[3]

"I really like all these ideas," the Marquise said. "I like these balloons that inflate and deflate every moment and these systems that are always in combat, and I especially like to see how this jostling makes an exchange of light between them, which assuredly is the only exchange they can have."

"No, no," I replied, "it's not the only one. The neighboring systems occasionally send us visitors, and they do it rather magnificently. They send us comets which are always adorned with dazzling hair, or a venerable beard, or a majestic tail."

"Ah, such emissaries," she laughed. "We could really do without their visit; it serves only to create fear."

"They only frighten children," I replied, "because of their extraordinary tails; but there are a great many children. The comets are merely planets that belong to a neighboring vortex. Their motion was toward the outer edges, but that vortex perhaps being differently compressed by those that surround it, is rounder on the top and flatter on the bottom, and it's from the bottom that we see it. Those planets which have begun to move in a circle at the top do not foresee that at the bottom they'll run out of vortex, because it's as if it were crushed there. To continue their circular motion they must enter into another vortex, which we'll suppose is ours, and cut across its outer edges. They also appear very high up to us; they move far beyond Saturn. It's absolutely necessary in our system, for reasons which have nothing to do with our present subject, that from Saturn to the two extremities of our vortex there should be a great void without planets. Our enemies incessantly reproach us with the uselessness of this great space. Let them no longer trouble themselves, for we've found a use for it; it's the dwelling of the alien planets that enter into our system."

"I understand," she said. "We don't allow them to enter the heart of our vortex with our planets; we receive them as the Sultan of Turkey receives the ambassadors who are sent to him. He doesn't give them the honor of lodging in Constantinople, but only in a suburb of the city."

"We also have this in common with the Ottomans," I answered, "that they receive ambassadors without sending any in return, and we don't send any of our planets to neighboring worlds."

"To judge by this," she replied, "we're awfully proud. Still, I don't know quite what to think of it. These alien planets have a very menacing air with their tails and beards, and perhaps they're sent to insult us, whereas ours, which aren't made in the same manner, wouldn't be so likely to create fear if they were to go into other systems."

"The tails and beards," I returned, "are nothing but pure illusions. The alien planets are no different from ours, but in entering our votex they take on the tail or beard from a certain kind of illumination which they receive from the Sun, and which, between us, hasn't been explained very well yet. We're sure that it comes merely from a kind of illumination; we'll figure it out when we can."

"Then I'd really like," she replied, "to see our Saturn go off with a beard or a tail to some other vortex and spread terror there, and then, having taken off this terrible disguise, return to its place here with the other planets and resume its ordinary functions."

"It would be better for it," I said, "never to leave our vortex. I've told you of the shock that occurs at the border where two vortices push and repel one another; I believe that in passing through there a poor planet is pretty violently shaken and its inhabitants don't bear it very well. We believe ourselves to be quite unfortunate when a comet appears to us; it's the comet itself which is most unfortunate."

"I don't believe that," said the Marquise. "It brings all its inhabitants to us in good health. Nothing is so delightful as to change vortices. We who never leave our vortex lead quite a boring life. If the inhabitants of a comet have wit enough to foresee the time of their passage into our world, those who've already made the voyage announce to the others what they'll see. 'You will soon discover a planet which has a great ring around it,' they may say in speaking of Saturn. 'You'll see another which has four little ones that follow it.' Maybe there are even people assigned to observe the moment when they enter our system and cry out at once 'New sun! New sun!' as our sailors cry 'Land! Land!'"

"Well I certainly can't hope," I told her, "to make you pity the inhabitants of a comet, but I hope at least that you'll grieve for those who live in some vortex where the sun expires and who remain in an eternal night."

"What," she cried, "suns expire?"

"Yes, without a doubt," I answered. "The Ancients saw fixed stars in the heavens which we no longer see. These suns have lost their light—assuredly great desolation in the whole vortex, widespread death on all the planets, for what can be done without a sun?"

"This idea is too grim," she replied. "Couldn't you have spared me this?"

"I'll tell you if you wish," I answered, "what some really clever people say: that these fixed stars which have disappeared aren't extinguished, that these are really only half-suns. In other words they have one half dark and the other lighted, and since they turn on themselves, they sometimes show us the luminous half and then we see them sometimes half dark, and then we don't see them at all.[4] I'll adopt this position to oblige you, since it's more palatable than the other, but I can only hold it in respect to certain stars which appear and disappear at regular times, as we've begun to perceive; otherwise the half-suns cannot be allowed. But what can we say of the stars that disappear and don't show themselves again after the time during which they would surely have been able to complete a revolution on their axes? You're too just to want to force me to believe that those are half-suns. However, I'll make another effort on your behalf. These suns won't be extinguished, they'll merely be swallowed up in the immense depths of the sky, and we'll no longer be able to see them. In that case the vortex will have followed its sun, and all will be well. It's true that the greater part of the fixed stars haven't this motion which takes them away from us; for at other times they would have to come nearer and we'd see them sometimes larger, sometimes smaller, which never happens. But we'll suppose that there are some few little vortices, more light and agile, which slip between the others and make certain trips, after which they return, while the majority of the vortices remain still. But here's a strange misfortune. There are fixed stars that show themselves to us, that spend a great deal of time appearing and disappearing, and then finally disappear completely. Half-suns would reappear at regular intervals; suns that sink into the sky should only disappear once and not reappear for a very long time. Make up your mind with courage, Madame: these stars must be suns which darken sufficiently to stop being visible to our eyes, and following that rekindle, and at last go out altogether."

"How can a sun darken and extinguish itself," asked the Marquise, "when it is itself a source of light?"

"The easiest thing in the world, according to Descartes," I answered. "Our Sun has spots. Whether these are scums or fogs, or whatever you please, these spots can thicken, join together, and adhere to one another; finally they'll form an ever-growing crust about the Sun and— goodbye Sun! We've barely escaped until now, they say. The Sun has been very pale for whole years at a time—during the one, for example, that followed the death of Caesar. It was the crust beginning to build. The strength of the Sun shattered and dissipated it, but if it had continued we'd have been lost."

"You make me tremble," said the Marquise. "Now that I know the consequences of the Sun's pallor, I believe that instead of going to my mirror each morning to see if I'm pale, I'll go look in the sky to see if the Sun is."

"Ah, Madame," I replied, "rest assured, it takes time to ruin a world."

"Nevertheless," she said, "isn't time all it takes?"

"I admit it," I said. "All of this immense mass of matter that makes up the universe is in perpetual motion; no part of it is entirely exempt, and the minute there's motion anywhere you can be sure change must come. It comes slowly or quickly, but always in an amount of time proportionate to the effect. The Ancients took pleasure in imagining that the celestial bodies were changeless by nature, because they'd never seen them change. Had they had time to prove it by experience? The Ancients were children compared to us. If roses, which live but a day, wrote histories and left memoirs for one another, the first would have pictured their gardener in a certain fashion, and after more than fifteen thousand rose generations those who had yet to leave the picture to their descendants would have changed nothing. They would say on the subject, 'we've always seen the same gardener; in all the memory of roses we've seen only him, and he's always been exactly as he is. Assuredly he doesn't die like us; he's changeless.' Would the roses' logic be sound? It would actually have more foundation than that of the Ancients concerning celestial bodies, and even though there'd been no change whatever in the skies until today, even though they gave every sign that they were made to last forever without any alteration, I wouldn't believe it yet. I'd wait for a still longer test. Should we make our lifetime, which is a mere instant, the measure of some other? Would that mean that whatever had lasted a hundred thousand times longer than we do must last forever? It's not so easy to be eternal. A thing would have to pass through many generations of man, one after the other, to begin to show some sign of immortality."

"Truly," the Marquise said, "I can see that systems are far from being able to lay claim to it. I wouldn't even give them the honor of being compared to the gardener who lasts so long with respect to the roses; they're more like roses themselves, living and dying one after the other in a garden, for I expect that if the ancient stars disappear, new ones will take their place. Species must replenish themselves."

"Have no fear that they perish," I replied. "Some people will tell us that these are merely suns that are returning to us after having been lost to us for a long time in the depths of heaven. Others will tell us that these are suns that have shaken off the dark crust that began to enclose them. I can easily believe all this, perhaps, but I also believe that the universe could have been made in such a way that it will form new suns from time to time. Why couldn't the proper matter to make a sun, after having been dispersed in many different places, reassemble at length in one certain place, and there lay the foundations of a new system? I've all the more inclination to believe in these new creations, because they correspond better to the high idea I have of the works of Nature. Would she have the secret of making grasses or plants or animals live and die in a continual cycle? I'm convinced, just as you are, that she practices this same secret on systems, and that it costs her no more effort."[5]

"Good heavens," said the Marquise, "I find now that the systems, the heavens, and the celestial bodies are so subject to change I've left them altogether and returned to Earth."

"Let's return even further," I replied, "if you'll believe me and speak of it no more. Besides, you've arrived at the last vault of the heavens, and to tell you if there are more stars beyond that, one would have to be more able than I am. You may put more systems there or not, it's up to you. They're properly the province of the philosophers, those great invisible countries that may be there or not as one wishes, or be whatever one wishes. I'm satisfied to have taken your mind as far as your eyes can see."

"Well!" she cried. "I have the whole system of the universe in my head! I'm a scholar!"

"Yes," I answered, "you are, well enough, and you've the advantage of being able to believe nothing at all of what I've told you, whenever you choose. I only ask of you, as payment for my trouble, that you never look at the Sun, the sky, or the stars, without thinking of me."

Notes

The Preface

1. Physics and astronomy made up Natural Philosophy in seventeenth-century England. See Prefatory comments, p. 1.

2. The phrase here "Je ne m'amuserai point," is particularly difficult to render in English. It had the sense of "repaître de vaines espérances."

To Monsieur L * * *

1. Monsieur L's identity is still unknown, and perhaps he is fictitious.

2. It has been said that the Marquise was Madame de La Mésangère, who enjoyed reading the draft of the work, but requested that Fontenelle make the resemblance less exact. Niderst has a detailed account, with logical conjecture, about this period in Fontenelle's life.

3. "Worlds," in this period, often if not invariably referred to solar systems, and will usually be translated as such in the following pages.

The First Evening

1. After 1687 Fontenelle changed this to read "and all the stars suns which light other worlds." As noted above, I will silently amend "worlds" to read "solar systems," when it seems appropriate.

2. I have capitalized nature when Fontenelle personifies it as the goddess, rather than the physical world around us.

3. The Great Bear or Big Dipper.

4. Literally here "self-interest."

5. A huge pastoral romance of over 5000 pages, written by Honoré d'Urfé. The first volume was published in 1610 and the last in 1627, finished by his secretary, Baro, after d'Urfé's death. It is essentially the amorous pursuit of Astrea by the shepherd Celadon.

6. Changed after the first edition to Castille, this must be a reference to Alfonso X the Learned of Castille and Leon (1252–84), an astronomer to whom the proposal was traditionally assigned.

7. In the 1714 edition, Fontenelle changed this to "more or less at the center," as a nod in the direction of Kepler's theory of elliptical orbits.

8. Fontenelle revised this passage in 1687 to 1703 editions to read "an immense turn around the Earth in twenty-four hours, that the fixed stars were in this great circle, where the movement is always the greatest, would run three hundred million leagues in a day, and go farther than from here to China in the time that one could pronounce the words, 'Go quickly to China'? For all this must happen if the Earth doesn't turn on itself in twenty-four hours. In truth, it's much more reasonable that it make this turn, which is no more than nine thousand leagues. Surely you see that nine thousand leagues in comparison with three hundred million is a mere bagatelle."

In the 1708 edition, he revised it yet again to read "an immense turn around the Earth in twenty-four hours, that the fixed stars which would be in this great sphere should run in one day more than twenty-seven thousand, six hundred and sixty times two hundred million leagues? Because all this must happen if the Earth doesn't turn on itself in twenty-four hours. Truly, it's much more reasonable that it make this turn, which is no more than nine thousand leagues. Surely you see that nine thousand leagues, in comparison to the horrific number that I just gave you, is a mere bagatelle."

An explanation for these changes is given by Shackleton, p. 183, n. 27.

9. A hypothetical country, perhaps Japan, somewhere in the northern Pacific Ocean.

10. The 1687 editions and those following omit the lines from here to "I want no more of this foolishness."

The Second Evening

1. John Glanvill substitutes London and Greenwich in *A Plurality of Worlds* (1688).

2. Fontenelle was using Descartes's theory here.

3. Shackleton points out in his 1955 edition of the *Entretiens* that Fontenelle here stays close to Wilkins's *Le Monde dans la lune* (1656).

4. In the 1742 edition Fontenelle changed this to dragon.

5. Fontenelle kept increasing the number of years correctly in subsequent editions.

6. John Glanvill alters this to "all the philosophers of Gresham."

7. In the 1687 editions, Fontenelle removed the passage from "All these" to "names of learned men," substituting "The illustrious Cassini, the one man in the world to whom the sky is best known, has discovered a certain object on the Moon that separates into two, is reunited, and loses itself in an area of holes. We can imagine ourselves, with some assurance, that it's a river. Finally, we know all these different places so well as to have given them names, and these are often the names of famous men." In the 1708 edition he altered the phrase which followed, "There are . . . Black Lake," to read: "One place is called Copernicus, another Archimedes, another Galileo, there is a Promontory of Dreams, a Sea of Rains, a Sea of Nectar, a Sea of Crises; . . ."

8. Glanvill changes this to "Mr. Flamstead himself cannot inform you."

9. *Orlando Furioso*. Fontenelle uses the alternate name Roland.

10. "The Donation of Constantine," proven fraudulent by Cardinal Nicolas de Cuse in 1431, and again discredited by Lorenzo Valla in 1440.

11. A potent inhalant made with denatured alcohol and rosemary. It was very fashionable and was supposed to relieve rheumatism and gout.

12. Shackleton points out that this sentence was struck from the 1728 edition in the Netherlands, and is the only revision in a foreign edition incorporated into the Paris editions by Fontenelle.

The Third Evening

1. Glanvill applies a bit of grim humor: "I could rejoice at a wreck," said the Countess, "as much as my neighbors on the coast of Essex."

2. Glanvill also changes this last phrase to read: "Cannot stay half so long in it, as one of the worst of Sir Harry Blount's sponge-gatherers."

3. Glanvill here inserts: "Nature hath as good a fancy as Mrs. Harrison," apparently an arbiter of taste in London at the time.

4. The 1687 editions and those following add the phrase "during days that are fifteen of ours" here.

5. In the 1687 edition and following, Fontenelle removed this sentence and added: "That world isn't completely exhausted," I answered. "You remember that since the two movements by which the Moon turns on herself and around us are equal, the former always presents to us what the latter would conceal, and therefore she always shows us the same face. Then it's only this half that we see, and since the Moon must be assumed not to turn on her axis in relation to us, this half that we see, sees us always fixed at the same place in the sky. When she's in night (and those nights are equivalent to fifteen of our days), she sees at first a little corner of the Earth lit, then a bit more, and nearly

hour by hour the light appears to her to expand on the face of the Earth until finally it covers it entirely; whereas the same changes appear to us to happen on the Moon from one night to another, because we lose sight of her for a long time. I'd like to be able to guess what poor conjectures philosophers make on that world, about why our Earth appears immobile to them, while all the other celestial bodies rise and set over their heads in fifteen days. They may attribute this immobility to its great size, for it's forty times bigger than the Moon [the edition of 1708 and following have sixty times]; and when the poets there want to praise their idle princes, I don't doubt that it serves them as an example of majestic reposes. One sees our world turn on its axis very plainly from the Moon. Imagine our Europe, our Asia, our America, which appear to them one after the other, very small and differently shaped, a bit as we see them on maps. How new this spectacle must appear to voyagers who travel from that half of the Moon which we never see to the one which we always see! Ah, how cautious their countrymen are about believing the first ones who've spoken of it, when they've returned to that great country where we are completely unknown!"

"It occurs to me," said the Marquise, "that from that other country to the one we see, people would make pilgrimages to view us, and that there would be honors and privileges for those who've seen the great planet once in their lives."

"At least," I replied, "those who see it have the privilege of being better lit during their nights; the population of the other half of the Moon must be much less comfortable in this regard. But, Madame, let's continue the voyage that we've undertaken from planet to planet; we've visited the Moon in enough detail."

6. Shackleton points out the sources of this "plenitude" theory in Cyrano de Bergerac, Sorel, and Pascal, and notes Leeuwenhoek's experiments with the early microscope (191–2).

7. The 1687 editions and following have "little fishes or serpents."

8. The 1708 edition and following drop "and the palate."

9. Through this whole preceding passage on "plenitude" theory, Glanvill translates by giving free rein to his imagination, with quite eloquent results (87–89).

10. The 1708 edition and following add "or tartar."

11. See Shackleton, 192, note 20, for an interesting comment on this passing reference to experience, meaning also experiment, four years before the publication of Locke's *Essay on Human Understanding*.

12. Shackleton points out that this following passage was inserted in 1742, and was inspired by J. B. Simon's *Le Gouvernement admirable; ou la Republique des abeilles* (1740): "Have I opened a wide enough field for you to exercise your imagination? Do you begin to see some inhabitants of planets?"

"Alas, no," she answered. "What you're telling me is marvelously empty and vague; I only see a great I-don't-know-what, in which I see nothing. I need something more definite, more distinctive."

"Well, then," I replied, "I'll resort to revealing every particular I know. It's a thing I have from a very good source, and you'll be convinced when I cite my authorities. Please listen with a little patience; this will be rather long.

"There are, on one planet that I haven't named for you yet, very lively, very industrious, very adoit inhabitants; they live only by pillage, like some of our Arabs, and it's their sole vice. For the rest, among them they have a perfect rapport, working together unceasingly for the good of the State, and above all their chastity is incomparable. It's true they don't deserve much credit for that; they're all sterile, no sex among them."

"But," the Marquise interrupted, "don't you suspect that you were being played for a fool when you were told this beautiful tale? How does this nation perpetuate itself?"

"I was not being played for a fool," I said in a cold tone. "All that I'm telling you is true, and the nation survives. They have a queen who never leads them to war, who apparently cares little for affairs of state, and whose royalty rests entirely on her fertility! She has thousands of children, and she does nothing else. She has a great palace partitioned into an infinite number of rooms, each of which has a cradle prepared for a little prince, and she gives birth in each of these chambers, one after the other, accompanied by a huge entourage who applaud her for this noble privilege which she enjoys to the exclusion of her people.

"I hear you, Madame, without your saying a word. You ask where she gets her lovers, or, to speak more honestly, her husbands. There are queens in the Orient and Africa who publicly have harems of men; this queen apparently has one, but makes a great mystery of it, and if that shows more modesty, it also operates with less dignity. Among these Arabs we're talking about, who are always busy whether at home or outside, one sees an extremely small number of foreigners, who look very like the natives of the country, but who are otherwise very lazy, who never go out, who do nothing, and who, to all appearances, wouldn't be tolerated among an extremely active people if they weren't destined for the pleasures of the queen, and the important mission of propagation. Actually, if despite their small number they're the fathers of the ten thousand children, more or less, that the queen brings into the world, they well deserve to be relieved of all other duties. What really persuades one that this has been their sole function is that as soon as it's been completely fulfilled, as soon as the queen has completed her ten thousand lyings-in, the Arabs, without mercy, kill those unfortunate strangers who've become useless to the State."

"Is that all?" said the Marquise. "Praise the Lord. Let's come back to common sense if we can. Where in all honesty have you taken all this fiction from? What poet supplied it to you?"

"I repeat," I told her, "that it's not fiction. All this happens here on our Earth, under your eyes. You're quite astonished—yes, under our eyes. My Arabs are simply bees, if you must know."

Then I taught her the natural history of bees, of which she knew hardly anything but the name.

"After this you can see," I continued, "that in merely transporting to other planets things that happen on our own, we could imagine bizarre things that would seem extravagant but could nevertheless be quite real, and we could imagine them without end, for after we've learned it, Madame, the story of insects is full of them."

"I can easily believe it," she answered. "Were there nothing but silkworms, which are more familiar to me than bees, they'd provide us with surprising enough people who would metamorphose into a completely new form, crawl during one part of their lives and fly during the other. Who knows? They might provide a hundred thousand other marvels that would make different characters, different costumes, for all these unknown inhabitants."

13. Here the 1742 insert ends.

The Fourth Evening

1. Shackleton and Calame both point out that the section of about eighteen lines which begins here was revised in editions after 1708, to portray Venus as 1½ times larger than Earth, and in 1742 as equal to Earth, although Regis had stated as early as 1681 that Venus was nearly equal to Earth (*Cours entier de philosophie*), and that this had been demonstrated in London in 1639.

2. At this point the editions again coincide.

3. Fontenelle once again couldn't resist poking fun at the idealized shepherds and shepherdesses of popular pastoral and romance, such as *L'Astrée*.

4. Editions after 1708 add this sentence: "It's about two-thirds the distance of Earth from the Sun." Glanvill adds a passage commenting on London gallantry, before this paragraph.

5. Editions from 1708 to 1724 add: "and they're two-and-a-half times closer to it than we are." The 1742 edition says simply: "They're more than twice as close to the Sun as we are."

6. Editions from 1708 to 1724 say: "more than six times as large," and the 1742 edition says: "more than nine times as large."

7. The following sentences are added to the 1714 edition and following editions: "Clearly our iron, our silver, our gold would melt there, and one would see them only as liquids, just as one sees water here mostly as a liquid, though at certain times it's a solid body. The people of Mercury wouldn't dream that on another world those liquids, which possibly make up their rivers, would be the hardest known substances."

8. The lines following, to the end of the paragraph, were removed from the 1708 edition onward.

9. From the 1708 edition onward this became: "a certain one is seventeen hundred times larger than the Earth, for you know that it's more than a million times smaller than the globe of the Sun."

10. From the 1708 edition onward the passage from "light" to "Finally" reads: "Others say, reasonably enough, that the spots, at least for the most part, aren't new entities which dissipate after a while, but great solid masses of irregular shape, always existent, which sometimes float on the liquid body of the Sun, sometimes submerge either entirely or in part, and show us different sizes and intensities according to how much or how little they're submerged, and what different sides they turn toward us. Perhaps they make up part of some great heap of solid matter which serves to fuel the fire of the Sun."

11. Again, from the 1708 edition onward there is an insert here, extending to "Now we must . . . ," reading: "and I'll tell you in passing that to go from here to there we've made a trip of thirty-three million leagues."

12. From the 1708 edition onward this becomes "a little more than half-an-hour longer."

13. Likewise, this becomes "two of our years, to within close to a month-and-a-half."

14. Editions from 1708 to 1724 make this "about four times smaller," and later, "five times smaller."

15. The 1708 edition is changed to "eight thousand times," and the 1724 edition changed again to "a thousand times."

16. Fontenelle changed this in the 1708 edition to "Mercury or Mars," following his changed opinion about the size of Venus.

17. In the 1708 edition, Fontenelle substituted: "It's five times farther from the Sun than we are, that is, a hundred and sixty-five million leagues, and consequently . . ."

18. In the 1708 edition, he also reduced the following passage, ending at "the prettiest sights in the world," to a much simpler statement. "The one closest to Jupiter makes its circle around it in forty-two hours, the second in three-and-a-half days, the third in seven, the fourth in seventeen, and by this inequality of their cycles they work together to give the prettiest sights in the world."

19. The 1714 edition and following read "sixteen hundred times."

20. In the 1708 edition, Fontenelle changed this to "four hundred times," and in the 1714 edition to "one hundred times." Shackleton reconstructs the reasoning behind the changes (p. 198, n. 31).

21. Glanvill adds Sir Francis Drake for his readers.

22. Cassini had discovered the fourth and fifth in 1684. See Fontenelle's revision of the following passage, immediately below.

23. In the 1708 edition, Fontenelle revised this passage, down to "and which," as follows: "and with ample justice because, since it revolves around the Sun in thirty years, it has countries where the night lasts fifteen years, for the same reason that the Earth, which turns around it in one year, has six-month nights under the poles. Saturn being twice as far from the Sun as Jupiter, and consequently ten times farther than us, would its five moons, so feebly lit, give enough light during the nights? No, it has another resource yet, singular

and unique in the universe. It's a great circle and a great ring large enough to surround it, and which . . ."

24. Shackleton points out that Fontenelle tactfully omits Plato's second point—for being male, not female.

The Fifth Evening

1. In the 1708 edition and afterward Fontenelle revised this ridiculously small figure to "twenty-seven thousand, six hundred and sixty times the distance from here to the Sun."

2. Such was the state of development of the telescope at this time. Fontenelle was expressing here a commonly held theory, derived from observation.

3. This, the famous theory of Descartes, so captivated Fontenelle that he adhered to it in the face of counterproposals by Newton and Varignon. Only the work of Villemot, which adapted Newtonian principles and the Cartesian theory, persuaded Fontenelle to adapt his own explanation, and in 1752 he was still so enamored of the subject that he published his own *Théorie des tourbillons cartésians*.

4. In the 1708 edition Fontenelle added this passage: "To all appearances, the fifth moon of Saturn is made like this, for during one part of its revolution one loses sight of it completely, and it's not because it would be any farther from the Earth; on the contrary, it's sometimes closer than at other times when we can see it. And although this moon is a planet, which naturally is of no consequence for a sun, one can well imagine a sun which would be covered by fixed spots, not like ours which has only transient ones."

5. Fontenelle had noted in 1706 that Maraldi had observed the appearance and disappearance of a new star. In the 1708 edition, he added this passage: "But we have more than simple conjecture on this. The fact is that during nearly one hundred years that we've been viewing with telescopes a sky totally new and unknown to the Ancients, there aren't many constellations where there hasn't been some perceptible change. It's in the Milky Way that we notice the most, as if in this swarm of little systems more movement and unrest prevail."

Designer:	U.C. Press Staff
Compositor:	Prestige Typography
Text:	10/13 Galliard
Display:	Galliard
Printer:	Edwards Bros.
Binder:	Edwards Bros.